welcome to witness

Witness is a study guide for the Sacrament of Confirmation. It contains material for both catechists and candidates and so offers a much fuller presentation of key aspects of our Catholic faith than is required for young people. Catechists can either select material for detailed study and leave the rest for private reading, or they may prefer to follow the suggested outline programme in the Appendix. The topic for each session is shown at the head of each page and the doctrinal points are clearly presented. Further background information and related topics are given in smaller print. Those involved in the R.C.I.A. programme, as well as parish faith study groups will also find in these pages material for reflection and discussion. We are called to witness to Christ every day of our lives. This is both a great privilege and an awesome responsibility. May we not be found wanting.

information for catechists...

Introduction

This teaching resource for Confirmation evolved over several years from a simple parish programme. Catechists are busy people with many demands on their time and they do not always have ready access to reference material. So when I was asked for more help and guidance with both the content and the presentation of the programme it seemed that something a little more  substantial was needed. I hope that *Witness* will prove to be sufficiently comprehensive for parish catechists to approach their important ministry with some degree of confidence. Throughout the book, reference is made to the relevant sections of the Catechism of the Catholic Church.

Catechists - leading others to Christ

During the whole time spent with the candidates, whatever their age, the aim must always be the same - to bring each person to a closer relationship with Jesus Christ, the Son of God, our Saviour and Redeemer. Everything else is secondary. This is truly preaching the Kingdom of Heaven. At the same time we know that we cannot hand on what we do not ourselves possess. We need to deepen our own faith commitment to Our Lord, by regular prayer and reception of the sacraments and to take whatever means we can to prepare for our apostolate. It is very important that catechists receive adequate training and support from the diocese and the parish. Distance learning courses are available, but lack of time may mean that the best practical help will come from within the parish community.

Ideally, there would be at least two or more experienced catechists in the team. It is good also to involve others who may wish to become involved but who may lack confidence. Retired teachers (especially experienced R.E teachers) have invaluable communication skills. Perhaps the "dream team" would include all of these together with the parish priest. The catechists must also be committed to attending each session. Confirmation is a sacrament of commitment; it would be very unfortunate if the catechists did not show a similar dedication.

Witness - an outline of the study guide

Witness is based loosely on the *Rite of Christian Initiation of Adults* and consists of three basic sections. The first of these is a time of enquiry, during which the candidates and catechists get to know each other and the candidates are asked some basic questions about themselves and the meaning and purpose of life. Then we look at the initial invitation of Baptism with its gift of the Holy Spirit, the presence of the Holy Spirit in the world and a revision of the dramatic events of Pentecost. If the candidates then decide that they wish to receive Confirmation, they are presented to the parish at a Sunday *Mass of Enrolment*. The priest welcomes them on behalf of the community and asks the parish to support their decision and to pray for them and their families and catechists.

The second part continues with a substantial element of religious instruction, much of which should already be familiar to the candidates. Once again, the overall purpose is not to give a revision course in the Faith but to help the candidates appreciate their Faith at a deeper level, so that they can decide to make a real commitment to the person of Jesus Christ the Son of God. This time of catechesis is described as a spiritual journey during which the candidates receive both guidance and information. The end of this part of the programme can be marked by a *Mass of Election*, or *Commitment* at which the candidates present their formal request to receive the Sacrament of Confirmation. Sample outlines of both these liturgies are given later in the book.

The third part of the preparation is concerned mainly with spiritual preparation for the sacrament. If possible it would include an overnight retreat or an 'away day' during which the candidates are given the opportunity to spend a quiet time together, to learn more about prayer, to examine their lives and receive the sacrament of Penance. It is a great blessing if the parish priest is able to celebrate Mass for all who are gathered for the retreat.

Preparation and Planning

Before beginning any arrangements, all members of the catechists' team will require clearance from COPCA and Criminal Records Bureau. This will normally be done through the parish Child Protection Representative and can take several months.

It goes without saying that the success of the meetings with candidates will depend largely on the time and effort spent in preparation. The team should aim to meet regularly and plan carefully the aim, both doctrinal or spiritual, of each session. Allow twice as much time for preparation as the length of each meeting and gather briefly after the meetings to assess how things went. Sometimes the meetings may take an entirely different direction from what was planned; the Holy Spirit may well be using your faith commitment to reach the candidates in a way you do not appreciate.

Bishops usually plan the confirmations a year in advance, so begin early and liaise with the parish priest. When deciding on the number of meetings, their dates, time, length and frequency, avoid clashes with school exams, half-term breaks, school and Bank Holidays; this can be a daunting challenge. Arrange the venue for the meetings and any details regarding availability and access. The age at which Confirmation is celebrated differs widely from one diocese to another. Some parishes write a personal letter to each potential candidate and their parents, inviting them to an introductory meeting. Others opt for a simpler approach and place a general invitation in the parish bulletin. They may also ask the headteacher to mention it at school assemblies for several weeks. This has the advantage of targeting those families who are more likely to attend Sunday Mass and so to appreciate the opportunity being offered by the Church.

"Catechesis is a fundamental element of Christian Initiation." (GDC No.66)

handing on the faith ...

First Meeting with candidates and their parents

The purpose of the meeting is to outline the meaning of Confirmation, to explain what is involved in preparing for the sacrament, to give out an information sheet and to answer any questions. When everyone has been welcomed, the catechists can introduce themselves briefly and each team member contribute to the presentation. A prepared text helps to avoid any nervous memory lapses. The faith and sincerity of the catechists is far more important than their ability to speak confidently in public. The meeting need only last about half an hour. The room should be warm and welcoming. The catechists, priest and helpers can greet the candidates with their parents or guardians and offer light refreshments while names and addresses are taken. Quiet background music helps put people at their ease.

Content of the Presentation

- Baptism, Confirmation and the Eucharist are called the Sacraments of Initiation. They complete our initiation into the Christian community.

- At Baptism our *parents* spoke for us and brought us to Christ. At Confirmation *our young people themselves* choose to follow Christ. If they are not yet ready, they can always ask to receive the sacrament later.

- We are marked/sealed by the Holy Spirit as disciples of Christ. We commit ourselves to witness to him. Our faith is strengthened and we receive the gifts of the Holy Spirit to witness to our Lord every day.

- Confirmation strengthens our friendship with Our Lord. This involves a mature commitment.

- Parents and the parish community should encouarge the young people by their prayers and good example.

- The liturgies of Enrolment and Commitment can be explained briefly at this point.

- Lastly, it is important to emphasize that regular attendance at Sunday Mass and at all the meetings is an essential part of the preparation.

Information Sheet

The following information should be available:

a) Names and telephone numbers of the parish priest and catechists.

b) Dates and times of the bishop's visit for Confirmation and of the church rehearsal.

c) Dates and times of the meetings.

d) Date, time and place of the retreat/away day with relevant information on travel arrangements, cost and parental consent forms.

e) The need for proof of baptism and details of how to obtain a certificate from another church.

f) The need to choose a sponsor early.

g) The dates and times of the Masses of Enrolment and Commitment.

Further Meetings with parents

Parents need our encouragement and support. A few briefing meetings are helpful to update them on the progress being made with their young candidates. If these are kept informal and informative, they can provide a valuable opportunity for parents to talk about their own faith and the concerns they may have. It could well be the first time that they have actually shared their feelings about religion and faith with anyone since they left school. Be ready to listen to them and affirm them.

Meetings with the candidates

Two or three sessions should be sufficient to cover the first section before the *Enrolment Mass*, and a further six to eight for the the main catechetical section. Two or three will probably be required after the *Commitment Mass*, if this includes a retreat period.

The catechists will need to decide on the sections they wish to work through in detail and which to to leave for background reading. Most of the significant sections for the candidates open with a prayer and this can be used at the beginning and end of each session. Each topic usually has more than one scripture quotation and this can be used for an opening period of quiet reflection and discussion before introducing the topic for the meeting. Some sections contain questions and suggestions to encourage the candidates to talk about their own faith and to make practical resolutions.

No two groups of candidates are ever the same. Young people are full of life and enthusiasm but many are at an age when they are experiencing dramatic changes within themselves. In addition to their physical, psychological, emotional and social development, their rapidly developing intellectual growth, with the beginnings of abstract and logical thought, makes for a confused and bewildered young person ready for some lively confrontation with parents and authority figures.

Decide on the length of the meetings; an hour should be quite long enough. From the outset everyone must realise that a prompt start means a prompt finish. Vary the routine to sustain interest, with small group discussions, visiting speakers if relevant, and maybe a selective use of power-point presentations, visual-aids and DVD's. Allow space at the end to relax with simple refreshments. Publish the time for collecting the candidates and do not keep the parents waiting.

We can learn much from young people. If we listen to them and respect their interests and enthusiasms and their culture we will gradually build up their confidence and respect. Above all, we must value their decision to find out more about their faith; they have shown courage and independence; they deserve our support and encouragement.

"Catechists bear special responsibility for the preparation of Confirmands." (CCC 1309)

LIFE A-Z

before we begin ...
what happens at the meetings?

Welcome to this book about our journey of faith.

What happens when we come to the meetings?

Before we start anything new, it helps if we have some idea of what to expect. One question young people often ask is "Will it be just like another lesson at school?" There will certainly be things to learn, but lots of the topics will be familiar to you already. Our time will be structured but it will be informal and relaxed. So there is nothing to worry about.

Once everyone has arrived and settled down, the session will usually open with a prayer and a short Gospel reading. This takes us into the topic for the meeting which the catechist will introduce. Quite often we will have an informal discussion, maybe in small groups, with a few questions to help us focus our ideas; a general session will gather our thoughts together and help us sum up what we have discovered. We can always find out more by checking out a few web sites. It is always useful to bring a biro with you and a note-pad.

If you are anxious about anything at all - e.g. you may have hearing or writing difficulties or may not be comfortable reading in front of others - just have a quiet word with one of the catechists beforehand. Never be shy about asking for help; you are with friends.

How can I get involved?

Here are a few suggestions:
- **Be faithful.** Come to Sunday Mass and Holy Communion every week.
- **Be committed.** Come to all the Confirmation meetings; no dodging.
- **Be courteous.** Be on time; every time.
- **Be friendly.** Make the effort to get to know each other.
- **Be respectful.** Respect others and be a good listener.
- **Be patient.** Not everyone can be as smart as you!
- **Be quiet,** when asked and especially at prayer time.
- **Be thoughtful.** Help with the clearing up afterwards.
- **Be grateful.** Others are giving up their time for you.
- **Be happy!** Share your happiness. Jesus loves us all.

How well do you know yourself?

We know that we are all unique; we know that God has given each one of us different gifts, talents and interests. Throughout our lives we will discover more and more things that interest us and that we enjoy, and we can spend a lifetime even in understanding ourselves properly, what makes us tick - let alone anyone else.

Why did you decide to come to this meeting?

When you arrived for this meeting were you:
a) Annoyed because your parents told you to come?
b) Reluctant or unwilling to get involved?
c) Shy? A bit nervous? Scared?
d) Relieved to see a few others you know from school?

Question time

How would you describe yourself? What kind of person are you? Read these one word descriptions and place a tick or cross beside them as you think they apply to you. Then you can ask someone else who knows you what they think. You could be in for a surprise.

I am:

kind	greedy	thoughtful	cheerful
stubborn	jealous	patient	grateful
quiet / shy	friendly	clever	lazy
helpful	attractive	polite	good listener
selfish	bully	reliable	impatient
rude	noisy	funny	boring

"The Church has need of the freshness of your faith." (John Paul II talks to young people)

Congratulations!

You want to find out more about the Sacrament of Confirmation. In Confirmation the Holy Spirit helps us become a close follower of Jesus Christ.

Let us Pray

Heavenly Father,
You love us and watch over us.
Help us with your Holy Spirit
to trust you and not to worry.
Help us to make the right choices in life
and to use your gifts to us.
We ask this through Christ Our Lord. Amen..

Becoming an adult

Many people receive the Sacrament of Confirmation while they are at secondary school or college. We all change as we grow older, it is part of our journey through life. Young people change very quickly and soon become independent adults. We change in lots of different ways - our appearance, physical growth, academic, artistic and sporting interests, our hobbies and our emotional relationships with others. All these things make being a young person a very special time, full of opportunities and challenges. Parents sometimes say "You have your whole life ahead of you - don't mess it up!" They know it is a wonderful, magical time; but they know that it has its own dangers and worries as well. They know that we will make lots of mistakes - everybody does; that is the way we all learn. We call it "experience". Here are a few things that young people sometimes find difficult to handle:

- You want to be independent but parents won't let go.
- You want to be treated as an adult but still feel a bit insecure.
- You want to decide things for yourself, but seem to make lots of mistakes.
- You have your own ideas about things and like to challenge grown-ups.
- Friends are important, so is street cred and being popular and cool.
- You have special gifts and interests that are unique to you.
- You need to know that others respect you.
- You begin to ask big questions about life - your future job or career.

What do you think?
"God is O.K. but religion is boring."

Some young people resent being nagged by parents to come to Mass with the family and may even have stopped going to church. They say that the Mass is boring and does not involve them or that the Church has lost the plot and its moral teachings are way out of date.

For others, Sunday Mass is very important. They want to be there to worship and thank God for his love. At Holy Communion time they can ask for help when they are anxious about things. They say that we have a duty to worship God even if we do feel bored at times.

a) Which of the above views do you share?

b) Do you really understand what happens at Mass?

c) Do you know why the Mass is so important?

d) Would you like to know more about the Mass and about Confirmation?

Confirmation helps us become adult Christians

Catholics believe that God loves us more than we can ever love ourselves. We all have special friends, but God is the most important friend we can ever have. He will never stop loving us, even if our other friends were to desert us. If we believe that Jesus Christ is the Son of God it changes the whole way we look at life. We really need to understand what Confirmation is all about and what a privilege it is to have received the gift of faith when we were baptised.

"Do not let people disregard you because you are young." (St Paul's 1st letter to Timothy)

LIFE A–Z

the journey of life

Life is full of new journeys and new experiences.

Setting off

We spend quite a lot of our day in travelling from one place to another. At first it will be going to school or college by bus or train, into town to meet friends or to a soccer match or pop concert. Later we will be travelling to work or to the supermarket or taking our family on holiday. Lots of these are routine and we do not think much of them. But sometimes our journey is special, even a bit scary. It could be a foreign trip for the first time, or an adventure holiday that will challenge us. We try to find out as much as we can beforehand so that we can be ready for whatever we meet.

Over to you

• Can you think of times you were a bit anxious about a journey?

• Have you ever been caught unprepared for a new experience?

• How would you get ready for a new challenge?
What if you were:

(a) starting a new school, (b) going solo on stage,
(c) playing in a music or drama group,
(d) reading in church, (e) going for a job interview,
(f) being picked for a sports team.

How would you prepare for these different situations?

Jesus leaves home for the first time

When Our Lord was only twelve years old, Mary and Joseph took him up to Jerusalem for a religious feast. Jesus stayed behind after they had started back to Nazareth in Galilee. When they realised that he was missing they were worried sick and when they found him, three days later back in the temple, Mary asked him:

"Child, why have you treated us like this? Look, your father and I have been searching for you in great anxiety. He said to them, 'Why were you searching for me? Did you not know that I must be in my Father's house?'"
(Read the whole story in Luke 2.41-51)

This story of a son who goes missing from home is a nightmare scenario for any family.

Jesus was just beginning to understand what his Heavenly Father was asking of him but his parents did not understand what he was talking about.

That is often the way when young people are growing up. Parents love us so much that they may seem over-protective at times. This can be irritating but parents are more alert to danger; they know that young people need security, respect and love. They need to talk and listen carefully to each other; there is a lot to learn. That is why Saint Luke tells us that Jesus returned home with his mum and dad and, as the Gospel says, "was obedient to them.".

A Pilgrim People

We are sometimes called a *Pilgrim People* because we are travelling along the road of life to our destination with God our Father in heaven. God took human nature in the person of Jesus Christ to teach us how to live and to sacrifice his life on the cross for our sins. People may say to each other " I love you to bits," but Jesus can say "I love you to death". This he did for us on Calvary. Now that he is risen from the dead he shares his life with us in the sacraments. He calls us to follow him. In Confirmation we are sealed with God's mark of ownership and receive the Holy Spirit to help us witness to him in our lives.

"The glory of the young is their strength." (Proverbs 20.2)

we need a map
to guide our way in life ...
Jesus is the Way

LIFE A-Z

Faith gives us a map of life

Young people at secondary school have to decide eventually what career, job or profession they want to aim at. Often the best advice is to choose something they find enjoyable or interesting, even though it may be difficult. We usually work best at the things we really enjoy. That way we are more likely to be happy and successful.

We all want to be happy

Most people spend their lives in search of happiness, success and fulfilment. Some find it in marriage or in the single state, or in their chosen job or career. All these situations involve working with other people. Life teaches us that we are social beings by nature; we need each other to help us develop as mature individuals. Our Lord showed us in his own life that love and the service of others is the only sure way to happiness. It all begins with our love for God and then for all our brothers and sisters who journey with us through this life to the next. Our faith gives us a map to follow in life - Jesus Christ.

Confirmation prepares us for our journey through life

Before we choose a map we have to know our destination, where we are going. We hear terrifying stories of people being lost in the mountains, desert or jungle. We can even get lost and confused in a large maze, but there are usually a few people around to help us.

The trouble about the journey of life is that there are always plenty of people who will show us the *wrong* way, leading us to do wrong and diverting us from our true destination - the happiness of God our Father in heaven. That is why the Sacrament of Confirmation is so important. When we are confirmed we receive the gift of the Holy Spirit to help us follow our Lord. Jesus is our map of life, as he said :.

> "I am the way, the truth and the life."
> (John 14.6)

Our Search for happiness

Nothing in this world, beautiful and full of wonder though it is, can give us complete contentment. This is because we are made to enjoy life for ever in heaven with God. We believe that God has created us to be happy and to have life to the full - both here and now and in the world to come when we die. Jesus often used the word *life* in his preaching:

> "I came that they may have life, and have it to the full."
> (John 10.10)

More Questions

- Do you think that money or riches can make you happy? If not, why not?
- Which is better - good health but no cash, or bad health and millions in the bank?
- What is more important - a really successful business or a really happy marriage?
- What is better - plenty of unscrupulous friends or few friends and your independence?

To sum up

Our search for happiness is really a search for God. Only God can fulfil our dreams. We can be certain of reaching complete happiness, peace in our hearts and fulfilment of our lives if we travel along life's road together with Jesus Christ the Son of God.

That is what Confirmation is all about.

> "You have made us, Lord, for yourself; and our hearts will find no rest until they rest in you."
> (St Augustine 354 - 430)

LIFE AZ

God has a plan for each one of us

A prayer about life

This thoughtful prayer about life gives us plenty to think about.
Let us read it slowly and then discuss each section afterwards.

1) *We are all created for God's glory - we are created to do his will.*
   I am created to do something or to be something for which no one else is created.
   I have a place in God's world, which no one else has: whether I be rich or poor,
   despised or esteemed, God knows me and calls me by my name.

2) *God has created me to give him some definite service.*
   He has committed some work to me which he has not committed to another.
   I have my mission - I may never know it in this life, but I shall be told in the next.
   Somehow I am necessary for his purpose. I have a great part in his work.

3) *I am a link in a chain, a bond of connection between persons.*
   He has not created me for nothing. I shall do good, I shall do his work;
   I shall be an angel of peace, a preacher of truth in my own place, while not
   intending it, if I do but keep his commandments and serve him in my calling.

4) *Therefore I will trust him. Whatever, wherever I am, I can never be thrown away.*
   If I am in sickness, my sickness will serve him; if I am in sorrow, my sorrow will serve him.
   He does nothing in vain: he may prolong life, he may shorten it.
   He knows what he is about.

5) *O Lord, I trust you wholly. You are wiser than I, more loving to me than I am to myself.*
   Fulfil in me your great purposes whatever they may be - work in and through me.
   I am born to serve you, to be yours, to be your instrument.
   I ask not to see: I ask not to know - I ask simply to be used.

(Cardinal John Henry Newman, 1801-1890 - a great Catholic scholar and writer)

1) We are all unique in God's world. God knows and loves me with infinite tenderness.
2) God calls me to do some special WORK for him during my life.
3) God calls me to WITNESS to him in my daily life.
4) God calls me to TRUST him completely no matter what may happen to me.
5) God has created me to know, love and serve him.
6) Find out more about John Henry Newman - check him out in Google.

"Jesus went through one town and village after another, teaching as he made his way to Jerusalem." (Luke 13.22)

signs and symbols ...
we meet God in the Sacraments

In this section we discover more about why we use signs in the sacraments.

Sign Language is not just for the hard of hearing

Sign language is a very important means of communication, but not just for those who are profoundly deaf; we all use hundreds of different signs and symbols every day.

The human race is a wondrous creation of Almighty God. We are made of both matter and spirit; we are part physical and part spiritual. Our physical body will surely die but our spiritual soul will live for ever. In the whole of creation, only human beings can think, speak, share thoughts, memories and dreams, love and touch each other at such rich and varied levels of intimacy. And so, within the family, we may kiss or hug our parents, children or married partner; but we are unlikely to greet the plumber or postman in the same way. We will speak to our class teacher or work supervisor in one way and then swop text messages with friends in another way.

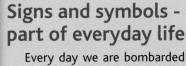

Signs and symbols - part of everyday life

Every day we are bombarded with all kinds of information - road signs, notices, T.V. ads, news bulletins, rail and airport announcements and food brand names or fashion logos. The spoken or written word is only one way in which we communicate with each other. Signs and symbols can help create an atmosphere, like beautiful art, majestic scenery or inspiring film or church music. In the commercial world, brisk music hurries us along at railway stations; calm music soothes our nerves before flight take-off or lulls us into a reckless buying spree in shopping precincts.

Much of the information we receive or give is by unspoken gestures, signs or symbols. These reinforce any message we may read, speak or hear. These signs are very important and very powerful. Some gestures can express an idea or an emotion that is very difficult to put into words. That is why the Sacraments use signs and symbols. They help us understand God's love for us.

Jesus uses signs and symbols

Jesus was a brilliant communicator. He reached people at their own level - young or old, rich or poor, simple or educated, social outcasts or sophisticated religious leaders. He was a master story teller; the parables combine a deceptively simple story from everyday life with challenging questions about fundamental choices we need to face.

He showed his divine power over sin and death when he healed the sick and raised the dead; he showed the dignity of humble service when he washed his disciples' feet. Whether he was walking on water, relaxing with friends, reading people's thoughts, writing in the sand, laying hands on children or fearlessly clearing the temple, Jesus was using a powerful sign language to make clear to the people the eternal truths of the Gospel. The most powerful of these signs was his triumphant death and glorious resurrection.

Signs of the Kingdom

Jesus did not work miracles just to impress the crowds, though these would certainly have strengthened their faith in him. To those who witnessed his miraculous powers, they were *signs* that the Kingdom of God had come. Saint John preferred to speak of Jesus' miracles as *signs*. When Jesus healed the paralysed man it was a sign that he had the power to forgive sin:

"But so that you may know that the Son of Man has authority on earth to forgive sins, he said to the one who was paralysed, 'I say to you, stand up and take your bed and go to your home.' Immediately he stood up before them, took what he had been lying on, and went to his home, glorifying God."
(Luke 5.24 - 25)

"As a social being, man needs signs and symbols to communicate with others." (CCC1146)

sacraments ...
signs of God's life in us

The Sacraments use signs and symbols to help us understand God's gifts to us.

What is so special about the signs used in the Sacraments?

Quite simply, the signs which the Church uses in the Sacraments are always powerfully effective. They are called *Effective Signs* because they always work. The Church uses signs and symbols to help us understand the spiritual gifts that we receive in the sacraments. They are given to us by Our Lord through his Church; and God cannot lie.

On the other hand, the signs we use in our daily lives are not guaranteed to work; we cannot always rely on them. For example, red traffic lights do not actually stop the traffic and they are often ignored. The door beneath an emergency EXIT sign may have been accidentally locked and hundreds could perish in a fire. Human signs can also tell cynical lies, like the terrible kiss of friendship with which Judas betrayed Our Lord in Gethsemane, or the false smiles and handshakes between sworn political enemies or world leaders.

Where does the word Sacrament come from?

In the early Church the word *mystery* was used to describe the way that God works in our lives. God's plan for us is a great mystery, as Jesus said:

> "To you it has been given to know the secrets (i.e. mysteries) of the kingdom of heaven, but to them it has not been given."
> (Matthew 13.11)

The word *Sacrament* was first used for the oath of loyalty made by a new recruit to the Roman army. Some were branded on the arm to discourage desertion. The early 3rd century Christian writer Tertullian translated the Greek word mystery as *sacrament*. He described Baptism as a *sacrament* because, like the enrolment of the soldier. Baptism is a permanent consecration to the service of God. This is brought about by the oath - the profession of faith made by the parents - with the visible sign, or brand which is the sign of the cross, the pouring of water and the anointing with chrism.

What is the difference between signs and symbols?

A sign: points the way or gives information. At Mass the consecrated bread and wine are visible signs of Christ's hidden presence.

A symbol: is a sign that points to a deeper, often religious truth that cannot be put simply into words but touches our heart and experience. Burning incense at Mass symbolises the sacredness of what is taking place and our prayers rising in praise and petition to God.

All symbols are signs but not all signs are symbols. Symbols are special types of sign; they point to a richer and deeper religious or spiritual truth.

Signs and Symbols used in the Sacraments

Baptism: The pouring of water, the sign of the cross and the anointing with chrism, the clothing with the white garment and the baptismal candle.

Confirmation: The laying on of hands, the anointing with chrism and the words "Be sealed with the gift of the Holy Spirit."

Holy Eucharist: The consecrated bread and wine.

Penance: The words of absolution and the sign of the cross.

Anointing: The laying on of hands with the anointing and prayers.

Marriage: The exchange of vows together with the exchange of rings.

Ordination: The laying on of hands with the anointing and prayers.

"Jesus illustrates his preaching with physical signs or symbolic gestures." (CCC1151)

baptism

1st Sacrament of Initiation (CCC 1212-1284)

Baptism, Confirmation and the Eucharist are called the Sacraments of Initiation.
They begin our special relationship with Our Lord.
To initiate means "to begin, to give basic instruction and information." (Oxford Dictionary)
In this section we take a closer look at the Sacrament of Baptism.

Let us Pray

Heavenly Father,
we thank you for the gift of faith.
In Baptism we become members of your family.
Help us to understand your love for us
and to witness to you every day.
We ask this through Christ Our Lord. Amen.

Jesus speaks of baptism as a re-birth

One night a Pharisee called Nicodemus came to see Jesus. He was a good man and he knew that Jesus came from God. Jesus told him:

"Very truly, I tell you, no one can see the kingdom of God without being born from above... Very truly, I tell you, no one can enter the kingdom of God without being born of water and Spirit."

(John 3.3,5)

Baptism is a spiritual rebirth into the life of God

During the Baptism, the priest reminds the parents and godparents that God is the author of all life, both human and divine. At Baptism we really begin to share in the life of Jesus. That is why it is called a re-birth.

Baptism brings us into the Church Community

When we are born we become a member of a human family and receive our family name. When we are baptised we become a member of another, much wider family, the worldwide Christian community. We are anointed as children of God and we receive our Christian name.

Baptism and Faith

At the beginning of his preaching mission Jesus and his disciples baptized people who wanted to change their lives and turn back to God. (John 3.22)

This was a preparation for the Sacrament of Baptism which Jesus was to leave us. Before he ascended to heaven, Jesus told his disciples:

"All authority in heaven and on earth has been given to me.
Go therefore and make disciples of all nations, baptizing them in the name of the Father and of the Son and of the Holy Spirit."
(Matthew 28.18-19)

At Baptism we receive the gifts of faith, hope and charity. But before anyone receives baptism, there must be a genuine sign of faith in the parents and godparents who speak on behalf of the infants.

Parents should be carefully prepared for the baptism of their children. They have a serious responsibility because they will be the first teachers of the Faith to the children.

As we grow older, our faith journey continues with the Sacrament of Confirmation when we say that we wish to grow closer to our Lord and to strengthen our faith by receiving the Holy Spirit.

The Church Teaches

Baptism is the basis of the whole Christian life, the gateway to life in the Spirit, the door which gives access to the other sacraments. Through Baptism we are freed from sin and reborn as sons and daughters of God; we become members of Christ, incorporated into the Church and made sharers in her mission. *(Cathechism of the Catholic Church 1213)*

This sacrament is called Baptism, after the central rite which is carried out: to baptise (Greek baptizein) means to 'plunge' or 'immerse'; the 'plunge' into the water symbolizes the person's burial into Christ's death, from which he rises up by resurrection with him as 'a new creature'. *(Cathechism of the Catholic Church 1214)*

Baptism is the Sacrament which cleanses us of original sin, makes us Christians, children of God and members of the Church. *(Catechism of Christian Doctrine Q 256)*

How did Baptism begin?

Centuries before the birth of Our Lord, the Jewish faith required people to wash thoroughly before prayer and before eating, because we are soiled or made unclean by our contact with the world.

Orthodox Jews still maintain a careful cleansing ritual before handling food and before eating and prayer. John the Baptist used this ceremony of ritual washing as a sign that people really wanted an inner cleansing of the sins that troubled their consciences so that they could prepare for the coming of the Messiah.

the sacrament of baptism

Why is baptism so important?

We know from our own experience that only too often we choose deliberately to do wrong instead of right, evil instead of good; we act against our conscience. Why do we behave in this way? Many have tried to explain this moral disorder or explain it away, saying that our feelings of guilt are negative and unhealthy. Faced with this evil tendency in human nature, the Catholic Church offers the doctrine of Original Sin.

Original Sin

The term Original Sin was first used in the early 5th century by Saint Augustine of Hippo (a town in North Africa). Augustine was one of the scholars who tried over many years to understand why it is that we choose so often to do wrong instead of right. Their explanation is still part of the Church's teaching.

In the beginning, mankind was created completely at peace and at one with his Creator. His human will was united to God's will and his instincts were controlled by his reason. Then, something went drastically wrong. Mankind disobeyed God, and rejected his friendship. This original fall from grace has weakened all of us since then. We are born in a state of original sin - though we are not personally responsible for the situation. The result is that we are created good - but flawed. That is why we all have to struggle to overcome our own weaknesses, faults and sins. As Saint Paul wrote: "I do not understand my own actions. For I do not do what I want, but I do the very thing I hate." *(Romans 7.15)*

The Symbolism of Water

We find that water is used to symbolise inner cleansing not only in Jewish and Christian spirituality but also in the Muslim faith where worshippers wash before prayers, and in the Hindu religion when people wash in the waters of the Ganges river.

The Bible is inspired. What does this mean?

The Bible is God's message to us. It was written down by ordinary people like ourselves, but what they wrote down was the message that God wanted them to write and what God wanted us to read. The Bible contains many different kinds of writing - history, wise sayings and proverbs, commandments and laws, prayers and religious songs and sermons or stories with a religious or spiritual message. Whatever kind of literary style is used, the human authors were inspired by God when they wrote. This is what we mean when we say the Bible is the inspired word of God. The Bible contains many important basic truths about life and about faith that God has told or revealed to us. (The Christian faith is a *revealed* religion.)

What can the Bible tell us about original sin?

In the early chapters of the book of Genesis (the first book of the Bible) we read the story of how the world began. This is similar to the creation myths found in other early civilizations but there is an important difference - the Genesis account has a deep religious message. This account of creation and of how mankind rejected the friendship of God was never intended to be scientifically accurate. It is simply a highly coloured presentation of some very important religious truths. This is what we learn from the early chapters of the book of Genesis.

- God is eternal. He has no beginning or end.
- God created the whole universe.
- God's creation is good.
- God made the human race as the very peak of his creation.
- At the beginning of human history, mankind chose freely to obey God's will and to enjoy his friendship.
- God's friendship was rejected when mankind refused to obey God.
- God punished mankind but promised to redeem his creation and bring us back to enjoy his friendship once more.

Original sin describes the time when mankind turned away from God and did not follow his will. When we are baptized we start our journey back to God's loving mercy; all our sins are washed away and we begin to share in the life and love of God.

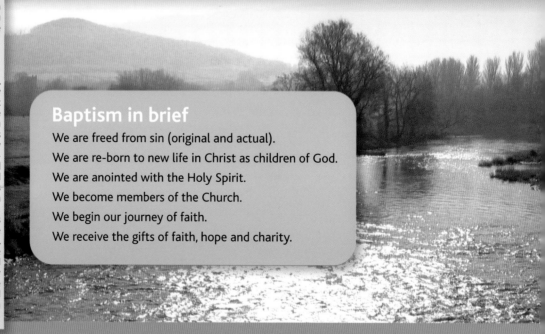

Baptism in brief

We are freed from sin (original and actual).

We are re-born to new life in Christ as children of God.

We are anointed with the Holy Spirit.

We become members of the Church.

We begin our journey of faith.

We receive the gifts of faith, hope and charity.

"Baptism ... erases original sin and turns a man back towards God." (CCC 405)

the rite of baptism

This outline of the rite of baptism reminds us how we begin our journey of faith.

The Reception of the child at the door of the church

The priest will have already met the family, either at their home or when they attend the preparation talks with the catechist at the church house. The first part of the celebration begins at the (inner) door of the church.

The parents are asked what name they have chosen for their child; then what they seek for their child and they reply *Baptism*. Parents and godparents are reminded of their duty to hand on the Faith by word and example and are asked if they clearly understand what this means.

The Sign of the Cross

The priest makes the sign of the cross on the child's forehead and invites the parents and godparents to repeat this. Since the 3rd century this has been used as a sign that a person now belongs to Christ.

The Celebration of God's word

The family with the godparents and friends are now invited to enter the church and to sit and listen to one or more readings from sacred scripture. These highlight the spiritual meaning of baptism as dying to sin and being born again to share in the risen life of our Lord. The priest may give a short homily on the readings, or he may prefer to explain the significance of each part of the rite as it occurs.

The Intercessions
(Bidding Prayers)

As with the Liturgy of the Word at Mass, so also here, following our meeting with Christ in his written word, we are now invited to pray especially for the child who is about to be baptized and for the parents and godparents.

The Exorcism and Anointing

The priest asks God to free the child from Satan, the spirit of evil and from original sin. The child is then anointed on the chest with the oil of catechumens. This is another symbol used in Baptism. Just as oil soothes, heals and protects, so almighty God will protect the child with his Holy Spirit.

The Blessing of the Baptismal Water

We now have a series of short prayers over the water which is to be used for baptism. These praise each person of the Blessed Trinity and ask Almighty God to help and guide those who are to be baptised so that they may live worthily as children of God. Our Lord chose water because it is a rich sign and symbol of his power at work in us. It represents the end of a life of sin and the beginning of a new life of faith.

i)   **Water cleanses dirt.**
     Baptism cleanses us of sin, both original sin in which we are born and also our personal sins.

ii) **Water can destroy life.**
     In Baptism we symbolically go down into the grave and die to sin.

iii) **Water also gives life.**
     In Baptism we are re-born as children of God and we share in the life of the risen Jesus.

Why begin at the church door?
Baptism marks the beginning of our life's journey to God. We begin at the church door because it leads us not just into the building itself but more importantly, into the community of the faithful, of which the child will soon become a member. So it symbolizes the family's wish for the child to be a member of this faith community.
These short introductory rites are sometimes celebrated at the beginning of a Sunday Mass, even some days before the baptism itself. This can be a happy way of welcoming the family and its new member into the parish family.

"Do you understand what you are undertaking?"
At several stages in the Baptism, parents and godparents are reminded of their duty to hand on the faith to their children. This is a serious commitment which should not be taken lightly. When choosing a name or names for their child, parents should include the name of a Christian saint.

Godparents
Godparents support the children and their parents in the Catholic faith. Social contacts and non-believers cannot fulfil this role; baptized non-Catholics can be included as Christian witnesses.

Readings and Bidding Prayers
This allows more of the family members to be involved in the celebration by taking an active part in the readings or bidding prayers.

Jesus - Priest, Prophet, King
These titles given to Jesus are from the Old Testament. Baptism calls us to follow our Lord in three ways:
As priest; Jesus sacrificed his life for us and rose again. We share in his priesthood by our prayer and worship. *(Dogmatic Constitution on the Church no 10)*
As prophet; Jesus spoke God's message. We are called to be prophets and bear witness to our faith.
As King, Jesus, Son of God, has authority over the whole universe. But his kingdom is not of this world; Jesus came to serve his people, not to be served by them. God's universal kingdom will come to perfection at the end of time. We are called to serve each other now like the Old Testament shepherd kings.

the rite of baptism

The Renunciation of sin and Profession of Faith

Three times the family is invited to reject Satan and evil. As we have seen, Baptism is a dying to sin and a spiritual rebirth into the life of the risen Lord Jesus. Everyone is then invited to profess their faith in God the Father, God the Son and God the Holy Spirit.

Who can Baptize?
A bishop, priest or deacon will usually baptize the children of Catholics. There can be situations when anyone can and should baptize a child. It is not uncommon for a premature baby to be baptized by a nurse in hospital if the child's life is in danger. This rite may not be repeated, but the priest will complete the other ceremonies, anointings and prayers at a later date when the baby is out of danger and the family are able to come to church.

Other forms of Baptism
There are two other main forms of baptism. These are situations which are taken as being equivalent to having received the sacrament.
1) Baptism of Desire. This refers to someone who sincerely wants to be baptized but who dies before being able to receive the sacrament.
2) Baptism by Blood. This refers to someone who is under instruction for baptism, but who is killed because he or she wants to become a Christian. This person would be a martyr.

How to baptize in an emergency
Pour water three times on the head of the person and say "N ... I baptize you in the name of the Father and of the Son and of the Holy Spirit. Amen."

Wrong reasons for baptism
Parents sometimes ask for Baptism for their children - but for the wrong reasons. Here are some of them:
1) "We need baptism to make sure of a place in the local Catholic Primary School.
2) "It brings good luck to the baby and the family."
3) "The grandparents will just keep nagging until we get it done."
4) "It is a great excuse for a party!"
5) "It has always been done in our family. I am not too sure why."

Candles
Candles are rich in *symbolism*. A lighted candle gives the same light, irrespective of its size, colour or shape. As Saint Paul reminds us, each of us is uniquely gifted but all our different gifts come from the same Holy Spirit, working in each of us in different ways. We can all share the light of Christ with others by the holiness of our lives. A burning candle is gradually dying as it gives out light. This reminds us of our Lord, whose whole life was poured out in loving service of us all, even to dying on the cross that we might live for ever with him.

The Baptism

The parents are asked a final time if they want their baby to be baptized. The water is then poured three times (in honour of the Blessed Trinity) over the head of the child as the priest says:

"N ... I baptize you in the name of the Father and of the Son and of the Holy Spirit. Amen."

The Anointing with Chrism

In Old Testament times, anointing was a sign that a person had been sealed, marked and chosen by God to do some special work. The same idea is present in the sacraments of baptism, confirmation and ordination. In the celebration of baptism the baby is now anointed with sweet smelling chrism as a sign that he or she is now specially chosen by God.

The Clothing with the White Garment

In the early Church, the adult converts were given a fresh robe as they came up from the water after their baptism by total immersion. Nowadays this form of baptism is not very common within the Catholic community. The white shawl or garment that is placed around the newly baptized baby reminds us of the purity of life to which we are all called. It is also a *symbol* that we have 'put on' Christ and are now clothed and wrapped in the love of God..

The Presentation of the Lighted candle

The Easter candle is a symbol that Jesus, the light of the world, is risen from the dead. It is usually located next to the baptismal font and it is lit for the celebration of baptism. The priest may now invite one of the godparents to light a small candle on behalf of the newly baptized child from the large Easter candle. This is a symbol that when we are baptized we begin to share in the life of the risen Christ The priest encourages the parents and godparents to keep the flame of faith alive in the child so that he/she may always walk in the light and love of our Lord.

The Closing Prayers and Blessing

The priest invites the parents and godparents (one of whom carries the lighted candle) to come to the front where they kneel or stand in front of the altar. He reminds them once more of the faith journey that awaits the child and after leading the Our Father he gives a special blessing to the parents before closing the celebration with a blessing for all who are present.

"baptizing them in the name of the Father and of the Son and of the Holy Spirit." (Matthew 28.19)

the sacraments of initiation -
an outline history

The Church teaches

"Christian Initiation is accomplished by three sacraments together: Baptism which is the beginning of new life, Confirmation which is the strengthening, and the Eucharist which nourishes the disciples with Christ's Body and Blood for his transformation into Christ."

(Catechism of the Catholic Church 1275)

For the first eight hundred years of Christianity (a period called the *patristic* age), the teaching of the Church is recorded in the Gospel accounts, the Acts of the Apostles, the apostolic letters and the writings of the early bishops, scholars and teachers, known collectively as the *Fathers of the Church*. From their many surviving documents we learn that the whole process of instruction and preparation to become a Christian was called the *Catechumenate*.

After a lengthy period of instruction the candidates were received into the Christian community at the Vigil of Easter. The bishop would baptize them, lay his hands on them and anoint them with chrism. They would be welcomed into the Christian community and they would receive Holy Communion at the first Mass of Easter. All this was celebrated as one single Rite of Initiation, not as three separate sacraments as we have now.

There was considerable variation in the liturgical ceremonies in different countries over this period. When Christianity became the official religion of the Roman Empire in the 4th century, the Faith spread rapidly and large numbers came for baptism. It soon became impracticable for the bishop to attend each initiation celebration, so priests would receive the converts, baptize them and anoint them with chrism which had already been blessed by the bishop. In the 5th century, Saint Augustine insisted on baptizing new born babies to save them from original sin and the fires of hell (this was not part of the Church's official teaching) so priests began baptizing children as soon after birth as possible.

The word Confirmation is not used in the New Testament. It first appeared in the 5th century. As Baptism became separated from the rest of the Rite of Initiation, the bishop would visit the local churches during the year and anoint the baptized Christians with chrism and the laying on of hands. This became known as Confirmation. Saint Patrick (c 389-461) wrote that he was the first person to bring Confirmation to Ireland. He also records that in Wales Confirmation was known as the bishop's baptism.

By the 13th century (the Middle Ages), Confirmation was seen as the sacrament of growth and was received at the age of fourteen, when young people could distinguish clearly between right and wrong.

For the next three hundred years it seems little preparation was done for these sacraments. In the 16th century the Protestant Reformers ignored Confirmation because it was not mentioned explicitly in the Bible. The Anglican Church now has infant Baptism, with Confirmation in young adulthood followed by first Communion.

From the 18th century to the present day the Catholic practice of Confirmation changed little, although it was still received before first Holy Communion. This changed dramatically in 1910 when Pope Saint Pius X encouraged children to receive Holy Communion at the age of seven - when they could appreciate the difference between ordinary bread and the consecrated host. The result of this was that the three original parts of the Rite of Initiation finally became independent of each other.

Catholics of mature years may reflect wryly on their childhood experiences when most of the sacramental preparation took place within the Catholic school. In due course, some fit or more candidates would be duly presented to the visiting bishop for Confirmation, often with a single sponsor. Recollections of these occasions may be tinged with some anxiety - lest nerves get the better of memory if asked a catechism question by the bishop; or concern lest the traditional tap on the cheek after confirmation be administered with undue episcopal vigour.

We can see a gradual change in emphasis in presenting this sacrament to the young. Several different ideas have been highlighted. These varied from becoming a soldier of Jesus Christ to receiving the Holy Spirit to combat the dangers to our faith, even as a rite of passage to Catholic adulthood. There was also considerable emphasis on memorizing Catholic doctrine in handy sound-bites. These ideas are all valid and are still present in varying degrees, but they have now merged into the realisation that Confirmation is an important stage in our journey of faith, at whatever age the sacrament is received. Our ongoing conversion and personal faith in Jesus Christ is nourished and strengthened by this sacrament within the community so that we can witness to our Faith before others. This approach is based on the Vatican II Council document, *The Constitution on the Sacred Liturgy* (1963), which encourages us to renew the link between these three sacraments. This is effectively carried out in the Church's Rite of Christian Initiation of Adults.

Christian Initiation

Baptism begins a new relationship with God the Father;
Holy Communion begins a new relationship with God the Son;
Confirmation deepens our relationship with God the Holy Spirit.

"And remember, I am with you always, to the end of the age." (Matthew 28.20)

the Holy Spirit ...

at work throughout creation (CCC 683 - 744)

The Holy Spirit is the third person of the Blessed Trinity.

The Holy Spirit is the infinite love and creative power of God.

The Holy Spirit is present throughout creation.

God is everywhere. He is closer to us than our own breath or the beat of our heart. We can be aware of his loving presence in the most unlikely situations. Some people are especially aware of the presence of God when they think about the awesome grandeur of the universe or when they are alone in the mountains or by the sea. Others know that God is close to them when they are broken with grief and cry out to him in anguish and desolation from their bed of pain. Others again may feel the presence of God in the sound of beautiful music or in the face of a child or in the understanding love of a friend. When people talk about their experience of the Holy Spirit, they are aware of a loving presence, calming and reassuring, full of consolation and hope.

The creative power of the Holy Spirit

At the beginning of the book of Genesis we read:

"... the Spirit of God swept over the face of
the waters." (Genesis 1.2)

"Then the Lord formed man from the dust of the ground, and breathed into him the breath of life." (Genesis 2.7)

In the New Testament we read how the angel Gabriel appeared to Our Lady and told her that she would become the mother of the Messiah by the power of the Holy Spirit:

"The angel said to her 'The Holy Spirit will come upon you, and the power of the Most High will overshadow you; therefore the child to be born will be holy; he will be called Son of God.'" (Luke 1.35)

The Bible uses symbols when speaking about the Holy Spirit

Three main symbols are used in the Bible to describe the powerful action of the Holy Spirit - *wind* or breath, *fire* and *water*. Let us look at each of these:

Wind or Breath:

If we blow up balloons until they burst or release them so that they whizz around the room we can see that our breath has given them a life and energy all their own, even though it is short lived. We know the frightening, destructive power of nature in a storm, tornado or tsunami. But we can also enjoy the invisible, refreshing coolness of a summer breeze and marvel at the birds as they playfully sweep and ride on the currents of air. In a spiritual way both strength, power and gentleness are present in the gift of the Holy Spirit. The Old Testament has one word - *RUAH* - for spirit, breath and wind. (The Greek word is *Pneuma* and the Latin *Spiritus*.)

Fire:

Like the wind, fire is also a great friend but a terrible enemy. It has immense power; it can destroy or harden, but it can also melt, transform, purify and cleanse. When Moses experienced the presence of God on Mount Horeb (Exodus 3.2) it was in the form of a burning bush. We shall see also that when the Holy Spirit came upon Our Lady and the Apostles at Pentecost, the visible signs were a powerful wind and tongues of fire.

Water:

As with wind and flame, so also with water; it can both destroy life and restore it. Water can put lives in danger at sea and by flooding on land. But water is also essential for life itself and in the waters of Baptism when we receive the life of Christ. Jesus speaks about the Holy Spirit in terms of refreshing water:

"Jesus cried out, 'Let anyone who is thirsty come to me, and let the one who believes in me drink. As the scripture has said, 'Out of the believer's heart shall flow rivers of living water.' Now he said this about the Spirit, which believers in him were to receive." (John 7.37 - 39)

"The Spirit of God swept over the face of the waters." (Genesis 1.2)

Jesus works
in the strength and power of the Holy Spirit

The Holy Spirit prepares Jesus for his mission

At his baptism, the Holy Spirit made clear to him the will of his heavenly Father:

"... When Jesus also had been baptized and was praying, the heaven was opened and the Holy Spirit descended upon him in bodily form like a dove. And a voice came from heaven, 'You are my Son, the Beloved; with you I am well pleased.'"
(Luke 3.21 - 22)

"Jesus, full of the Holy Spirit, returned from the Jordan and was led by the Spirit in the wilderness, where for forty days he was tempted by the devil."
(Luke 4.1 - 2)

Jesus proclaims the Good News in the power of the Holy Spirit

After his time in the wilderness, Jesus returned to Galilee and began preaching the Kingdom of God. In his home synagogue in Nazareth he read this passage from the prophet Isaiah:

"The Spirit of the Lord is upon me, because he has anointed me to bring the good news to the poor. He has sent me to proclaim release to the captives and recovery of sight to the blind, to let the oppressed go free' ...Then he began to say to them, 'Today this scripture has been fulfilled in your hearing.'"
(Luke 4.18 - 21)

Everyone was amazed at the way Jesus spoke - with calm wisdom and deep knowledge of the scriptures. But their admiration turned sour when they could not accept that he came from God and is their king and long-awaited Messiah.

Jesus reassures his disciples

Jesus told his followers never to be afraid of preaching the Gospel:

"When they take you before synagogues and magistrates and authorities,do not worry about how to defend yourselves or what to say, because when the time comes, the Holy Spirit will teach you what you should say." (Luke 12.11 - 12)

At his Last Supper, Jesus spent time encouraging his disciples. He reassured them that once he had risen from the dead, they would receive the Holy Spirit. He repeated this message:

"If you ask me anything in my name, I will do it ... I shall ask the Father, and He will send you another Paraclete (advocate) to be with you for ever ... I have said these things to you while still with you; but the Paraclete, the Holy Spirit, whom the Father will send in my name, will teach you everything and remind you of all I have said to you."
(John 14.13-26)

Before his Ascension, Jesus again promises that the Holy Spirit will come

On several occasions, shortly before he ascended to his Heavenly Father, Jesus gave clear instructions to his disciples. He told them to preach the Gospel to all nations and to baptize them in the name of the Father and of the Son and of the Holy Spirit. (Matthew 28.19) He said that the Holy Spirit would give them power to preach in his name:

"And now I am sending upon you what the Father has promised. Stay in the city, then, until you are clothed with power from on high."
(Luke 24.49)

"... John baptized with water, but you will be baptized with the Holy Spirit, not many days from now ... you will receive power when the Holy Spirit has come upon you; and you will be my witnesses in Jerusalem, in all Judaea and Samaria, and to the ends of the earth."
(Acts 1.5,8)

pentecost ...
the Holy Spirit comes
upon the Apostles

The Holy Spirit came upon the Apostles with a mighty wind and tongues of fire. They were transformed and began to preach the Gospel with courage and conviction.

Pentecost

Pentecost was a Jewish Thanks-giving Festival at the end of the grain harvest. Originally known as the Feast of Weeks, it was celebrated 7 weeks after the Feast of Passover. Pentecost later commemorated the giving of the Ten Commandments to Moses on Mount Sinai.

Catholics celebrate Pentecost fifty days after Easter, the day that the Holy Spirit came down upon the Apostles. Pentecost is the birthday of the Church. Pentecost is sometimes called Whit Sunday because those who had been baptized at Easter wore their white baptismal robes in public processions of Catholic witness through the town. Later it was an occasion for the first Holy Communion children to walk in procession dressed in white.

Whit Walks

By the mid nineteenth century, the Catholic hierarchy was being legally re-introduced in the U.K. after over three hundred years of persecution and prejudice. The Pentecost or Whit Sunday processions (Generally known as the Whit Walks) on a Bank Holiday weekend became popular in towns and cities throughout the country, especially where there was a large Catholic population. These sometimes included the carrying of the Blessed Sacrament. For many years they were an important and powerful expression of faith for a Catholic community which had only recently achieved national emancipation. The wider community was able to see the strength of faith and commitment of so many hard working families in the town. They became a popular event in the local calendar, though not without opposition in some areas. The processions were colourful and happy occasions as the school children and teachers, clergy and altar servers, members of the Catholic societies confraternities, sodalities, and the scout and guide movement, walked through the streets behind their banners, and singing hymns to the accompaniment of marching bands.

Pentecost - the Holy Spirit comes down upon the Apostles

The Apostles, Our Lady and a few close friends gathered in Jerusalem, as Jesus had told them, to wait for the coming of the Holy Spirit. They were anxious lest they be arrested by those who had called for the death of Jesus:

> "When Pentecost day came round, they had all met together, when suddenly there came from heaven a sound as of a violent wind which filled the entire house in which they were sitting;
> and there appeared to them tongues as of fire; these separated and came to rest on the head of each of them. They were filled with the Holy Spirit and began to speak different languages as the Spirit gave them power to express themselves."
> (Acts 2.1-4)

The Apostles are changed by the Holy Spirit

Pentecost was a dramatic manifestation of the loving power of the Holy Spirit. Read the first chapters of Acts for a first hand account.

- They spoke different languages - the Gospel message is for everyone.
- They were no longer afraid and preached with courage and conviction.
- They understood the scriptures - especially the prophecies about Jesus.
- They understood the teachings of Jesus - especially about the Kingdom

Peter and John proclaim the Gospel before the Council of Elders

One day, Peter cured a man 'in the name of Jesus Christ of Nazareth'. The crowds were amazed and Peter and John urged them to repent and turn back to God. The temple authorities were annoyed; they had the apostles arrested for preaching that Jesus had risen from the dead. They were brought before the council of priests, elders and scribes - the men who had condemned Jesus to death for blasphemy. Peter and John were told to explain themselves:

> "Then Peter, filled with the Holy Spirit, said to them, ' Rulers of the people and elders ...let it be known to all of you ... that this man isstanding before you in good health by the name of Jesus Christ of Nazareth, whom you crucified, whom God raised from the dead...
> There is salvation in no one else, for there is no other name under heaven given among mortals by which we must be saved.' Now when they saw the boldness of Peter and John and realized that they were uneducated and ordinary men, they were amazed and recognized them as companions of Jesus." (Acts 4.8 - 13)

Before they were released, Peter and John were forbidden to speak of Jesus, but replied that they could not possibly stop speaking about what they had experienced. A few days later, they were again arrested and thrown into prison. They were miraculously released and continued preaching in public, only to be rearrested and brought once more before the council. They defended their actions:

> "Peter and the apostles answered; 'We must obey God rather than any human authority. The God of our ancestors raised up Jesus, whom you had killed by hanging him on a tree. God exalted him at his right hand as Leader and Saviour that he might give repentance to Israel and forgiveness of sins. And we are witnesses to these things, and so is the Holy Spirit, whom God has given to those who obey him."
> (Acts 5.29 - 32)

"All of them were filled with the Holy Spirit and began to speak in other languages." (Acts 2.4)

confirmation

2nd Sacrament of Initiation (CCC 1285 - 1321)

The Holy Spirit came down upon the apostles at Pentecost. Confirmation is the sacrament in which we receive the gift of the same Holy Spirit.

Let us Pray

*Come, Holy Spirit, fill the hearts of your faithful
and enkindle in them the fire of your love.
Send forth your spirit and they shall be created
and you shall renew the face of the earth.
O God who taught the hearts of the faithful by the light of
the Holy Spirit, grant that by the gift of the same Spirit
we may be always truly wise and ever rejoice in his
consolation through Christ Our Lord, Amen.*

What is special about the Sacrament of Confirmation?

- Confirmation, Baptism and the Eucharist are sacraments of initiation.
- The sacraments of initiation make us full members of the Church.
- Confirmation seals, confirms and perfects what we received at Baptism.
- Confirmation gives us grace to witness to our faith in word and deed.
- Confirmation helps us take responsibility to help build up the Church.

Will we notice any difference after we have been confirmed?

The best answer to this question is: " It very much depends on what we are expecting." We will not suddenly become a brilliant soccer player, pop-star or millionaire business tycoon.

Confirmation is not about worldly success; it is much more fundamental than that. It is about becoming closer to Our Lord, and becoming an active member of the Church. Confirmation calls us to live our faith with joy and conviction so that we can draw others to the love and friendship of Our Lord. But we have to be prepared to change and that can be tough. Saint Paul wrote to the early Christians:

"Do not be conformed to this world, but be transformed by the renewing of your minds, so that you may discern what is the will of God - what is good and acceptable and perfect."
(Romans 12.2)

"Be very careful about the sort of lives you lead, like intelligent and not senseless people. This may be a wicked age, but your lives should redeem it. And do not be thoughtless but recognize the will of the Lord."
(Ephesians 5.15 - 17)

Talking points

The grace of the Holy Spirit helps us witness to our Lord. Here are a few practical ideas. How can you get involved in any of these situations?

- We can put God first in our lives; we can pray for courage and wisdom.
- We can follow our conscience, not just follow the crowd.
- We can stand up for our faith and speak out in defence of the truth.
- We can be more thoughtful and kind to people in need.
- We can do more at college or work to raise awareness of world poverty.
- We can become involved at a local level with the Society of Saint Vincent de Paul, with Cafod and with pro-life organisations like the Society for the Protection of the Unborn Child (SPUC).

The Church Teaches

"The essential rite of Confirmation is anointing theforehead of the baptized with sacred chrism, together with the laying on of the minister's hand and the words: Be sealed with the Gift of the Holy Spirit". *(Catechism of the Catholic Church 1320)*

"By the sacrament of Confirmation, the baptized are more perfectly bound to the Church and are enriched with a special strength of the Holy Spirit. Hence they are, as true witnesses of Christ, more strictly obliged to spread and defend the faith by word and deed." *(Catechism of the Catholic Church 1285)*

"The imposition of hands is rightly recognized by the Catholic tradition as the origin of the sacrament of Confirmation, which in a certain way perpetuates the grace of Pentecost in the Church." *(Paul VI quoted in Catechism of the Catholic Church 1288)*

What does the word Paraclete mean?

This Greek word is used mainly in a legal context of a person who helps someone, or speaks on their behalf. When it is used (only five times) in the New Testament, it is used of Jesus who is our intercessor or advocate with the Father (1 John 2.1). At the Last Supper, Jesus himself promises that the Father will send another *Advocate*, the *Spirit of truth*. (John 14.16 and 15.26). Shortly after this, Jesus speaks of the Advocate as the *Holy Spirit*. (John 14.26 and 16). So the Paraclete is the Holy Spirit who will make things clear to the disciples. The same Holy Spirit, the Third Person of the Blessed Trinity, will help us bear witness to our Faith.

the gifts and fruits of the Holy Spirit

At Confirmation, the bishop prays that the Holy Spirit will be our helper and guide. The Church tells us about the gifts and fruits of the Spirit.

Gifts

What do you do when you receive a surprise gift? Do you

i)   Open it at once and thank the donor?

ii)   Tell them you may look at it later?

iii)   Say you do not want it and reject it?

The best thing to do is to open it in front of the donor and thank them for their kindness. When young children are given a present of sweets, they are reminded to say 'thank you' and to offer them to others first of all. This reminds us of an important truth; gifts are meant to be shared with others. The same is true of the gifts of the Holy Spirit we receive at Baptism and Confirmation. They are given to us to use for the building up of our community of faith.

The Seven Gifts of the Holy Spirit

The Old Testament prophet Isaiah speaks of special gifts that the Lord will bestow on a descendant of Jesse (the father of King David). Christians believe that Isaiah was speaking about the coming Messiah, Jesus Christ, who is a descendant of King David:

"A shoot shall come out from the stock of Jesse, and a branch shall grow out of his roots. The spirit of wisdom and understanding, the spirit of counsel and might, the spirit of knowledge and the fear of the Lord." (Isaiah 11.1-2)

We receive these same gifts of the Holy Spirit when we are confirmed. They help us in different ways:

Wisdom	helps us to put God's will first when we are faced with big decisions.
Understanding	helps us understand the Gospel and the truths of our Faith.
Right Judgment	(Counsel) helps us choose good over evil in difficult situations.
Courage	(Fortitude) helps us do what is right despite mockery or criticism.
Knowledge	helps us judge everyday situations with eyes of faith.
Reverence	(Piety) helps us always to honour God and respect other people.
Wonder and Awe	(Fear of the Lord) helps respect and love the awesome presence of God.

Saint Paul writes about the gifts we receive from the Holy Spirit

Saint Paul reminds us that we are all gifted in many different ways. Our gifts are best when they are shared. Our gifts of mind and spirit can help to support each other on our journey through life:

"Now there are varieties of gifts, but the same Spirit; and there are varieties of services, but the same Lord; and there are varieties of activities, but it is the same God who activates all of them in everyone. To each is given the manifestation of the Spirit for the common good. To one is given through the Spirit the utterance of wisdom, and to another the utterance of knowledge according to the same Spirit, to another faith by the same Spirit, to another gifts of healing by the one Spirit, to another the working of miracles, to another prophecy, to another the discernment of spirits, to another various kinds of tongues, to another the interpretation of tongues. All these are activated by one and the same Spirit, who allots to each one individually just as the Spirit chooses."

(1 Corinthians 12.4-11)

The gifts we receive from the Holy Spirit at Confirmation are like seeds. We need to feed them with prayer and use them so that they can grow and develop within us and we can gradually become the mature and joyful people that God wishes us to be.

"There are varieties of gifts, but the same Spirit." (I Corinthians 12.4)

the gifts and fruits of the Holy Spirit

God calls us to love our neighbour by sharing our gifts with others. We can use all our gifts to witness to Christ and to serve each other.

Talking points - what are my gifts?

As Saint Paul reminded us we are all gifted by God in many different ways, irrespective of our age. Some are gifted artistically - art, music, singing or drama and dance. Others are great at sports, P.E. or all kinds of practical craft work in wood and metal or with computers and electronics. Others again are really good at languages, science, maths, history, geography or RE. We discover our gifts and talents as we grow older; but what gifts and talents can you recognize in yourself at the moment? Make a list of them or share them with each other.

a) Gifts and talents you know you have - usually things you can do well and enjoy.

b) Gifts and talents you can use for others or share with others.

c) Gifts and talents you know you have but have not yet bothered to develop.

d) Are there any gifts you wish you had?

Life can be tough for all of us whatever our age. Bullying or peer pressure in some form or other can be as common in the work place as in school or college. We can be expected to follow the crowd, whether in fashion, behaviour, language, doing drugs, drink or casual sex. The grace of God at Confirmation helps us make the right decisions, though we may not always be popular.

Then there may well be other things about ourselves that upset or embarrass us. Often we may grow out of them; others may be with us for life. It could be spots, acne, dandruff, greasy hair, freckles, bad breath, teeth braces or smelly feet! Some people are very shy and blush easily, others always seem to struggle to cope with studies, others are deaf, dyslexic, asthmatic, overweight or very short - sighted.

The important thing to remember is that, whatever we look like or whatever we have to struggle with, none of these situations is the REAL me inside. God knows us through and through and he loves us just as we are, in our uniqueness. That is what we must always remember.

The Twelve Fruits of the Holy Spirit

We can tell what people are like by their 'fruits' - by the way they behave.

As we grow older we change and mature. We learn our good qualities and our weaknesses.

The Holy Spirit is within us from our Baptism and in Confirmation the Holy Spirit gives us extra strength to choose good and avoid evil and sin. But we are still free to decide which way we want to go and sometimes we choose the wrong way. Saint Paul gives some strong advice to the young Christians in Galatia (modern Turkey). At the end he identifies good qualities which he describes as the Fruits of the Spirit:

"Live by the Spirit, I say, and do not gratify the desires of the flesh ... Now the works of the flesh are obvious: fornication, impurity, licentiousness, idolatry, sorcery, enmities, strife, jealousy, anger, quarrels, dissensions, faction, envy, drunkenness, carousing and things like these. I am warning you, as I have warned you before; those who do such things will not inherit the kingdom of God. By contrast, the fruit of the spirit is: **love, joy, peace, patience, kindness, generosity, faithfulness, gentleness and self-control ...** If we live by the Spirit, let us also be guided by the Spirit."
(Galatians 5.16-25)

The Church has added to this list and given us twelve ways we can reflect God's love. These are:

Charity, Joy, Peace, Patience, Kindness, Goodness, Generosity, Gentleness, Faithfulness, Modesty, Self-control, Chastity.

Several of the gifts and fruits of the Holy Spirit mentioned here are very similar to each other. They are just some of the things we will notice about a person who is close to God.

things to do
before confirmation

As we begin to prepare for Confirmation, we need to check out a few details.
(a) proof of Baptism, (b) decision on a Confirmation name, (c) choice of a Sponsor.

(a) Proof of Baptism

This is a simple form, called a Baptismal Certificate, which is issued by the church of your Baptism. It is a copy of the information about you that is held in the church's baptism register. Check first with your parish priest. If you have moved since you were baptized, you will need to contact the priest at the church of your baptism and ask for a copy of your baptism details. Make sure that you give as much information as possible - full names of yourself, your parents and godparents, the date of your birth and baptism and your home address at the time. If you write for this information, include a stamped, addressed envelope; this helps to ensure a prompt reply.

(b) Confirmation name

In the Bible we read that God gave a new name to a person when given a special task to fulfil. For example, when God called Abram away from his tribe and promised to make his descendants into a great nation, he renamed him Abraham (Genesis 17.5). When Jesus gave special authority to Simon he renamed him Peter. (Matthew 16.18) In Acts of Apostles we read that Saul was called Paul after his conversion. (Acts 13.9)

When we receive the Holy Spirit at Confirmation we are making a mature decision to offer our life to God; and the gifts we receive will help us to bear witness to Our Lord. To mark this important decision we can take an extra name. We should choose only a recognized saint, someone we admire; then we can learn about their life and pray to them for help and guidance.

But we do not have to choose an extra name at our Confirmation. The Church encourages us to use our baptismal name because it reminds us that Confirmation is linked to the sacrament of Baptism. At confirmation we re-affirm the choice that our parents made for us at our baptism.

(c) What is a Sponsor?
What does a Sponsor do?

You will need to choose someone to sponsor you for your Confirmation. A Sponsor is an adult who continues the work of a godparent at Baptism. The sponsor presents you to the bishop on behalf of the parish community. This is not just a friendly gesture of support. It means that your sponsor believes you to be a mature person, ready to make a serious commitment of faith as a member of this Catholic community; and that you are a suitable candidate for the Sacrament of Confirmation. The duties of a sponsor are:

• to help you to live as a true witness of Our Lord,

• to help you take your faith seriously,

• to support you with prayer, encouragement and good example,

• to speak up for you on behalf of the parish and present you to the bishop.

Who can be my Sponsor?

The ideal is for one of your baptismal god - parents to be your Confirmation sponsor. Parents do not usually sponsor their own children. An older family relative, even a brother or sister could be your sponsor. It is very important that your sponsor fulfil the required conditions:

• to speak up for you on behalf of the parish and present you to the bishop.

• Someone who knows you well and is -

• at least sixteen years of age,

• baptized and confirmed in the Catholic Church,

• a practising member of the church community.

Prayer friend

Individual parishioners may be invited to 'adopt' a particular candidate for Baptism or Confirmation and to pray for them during their time of preparation. This helps the whole parish to appreciate the important step that the candidates are taking. It is also a valuable reminder that we all rely on the prayers of our brothers and sisters in the parish community.

Confirmation requires (a) proof of Baptism, (b) a Confirmation name, (c) a Sponsor.

the confirmation mass

Presentation of the Candidates

The bishop is the spiritual father of the diocese.

He visits each parish to administer the Sacrament of Confirmation.

In this section we look at our celebration of the parish Confirmation Mass.

Introduction

Confirmation is normally celebrated within Mass. Wherever possible, the entry procession is led by the thurifer, cross bearer and acolytes. These are followed by other servers and ministers of the Word, parish clergy and the bishop with his assistants. It is good if young people, though not the candidates, can be involved with the music and leading the singing. The liturgy will be longer than usual so not everything should be sung, but the choice of music should allow the whole parish community to celebrate in song. Copyright permission must always be obtained before printing an Order of Service. When planning the liturgy it is both courteous and prudent to check the proposed outline of the liturgy with the parish priest. Be prepared to make any necessary changes. For example, the bishop may wish to confirm the candidates without any accompanying music or singing - so that all can hear the sacrament being conferred.

The Mass begins

When the procession arrives at the sanctuary, the altar is incensed, the bishop greets the people and Mass begins with the Penitential Rite, Glory to God, opening prayer and Liturgy of the Word. After the Gospel, the bishop comes forward and takes his seat at the front of the altar, ready for the rite of Confirmation.

The candidates will usually sit either together at the front of the church or with their own family. Each candidate may sit at the end of a bench next to the central aisle, beside the sponsor, with the rest of the family seated next to them and in the row behind. There will be a rehearsal a few days before the celebration, so that everyone involved can become familiar with the reserved seating arrangements and their responsibilities.

The Presentation of the Candidates

The priest, deacon or one of the catechists now presents the candidates to the bishop:

"My Lord Bishop, I wish to present to you the following candidates for the sacrament of Confirmation from the parish of .... They have been preparing by prayer and study and are now ready to come before you and before the people of this parish."

The names of the candidates are then read out and the bishop may expect you to stand as your name is called. When everybody has been introduced, you will be invited to sit for the homily.

The Homily

In his homily, the bishop will talk about the events of Pentecost when the Apostles received the Holy Spirit and the Church community was born. He will also encourage the candidates to bear witness to Our Lord each day and to ask the Holy Spirit for strength and guidance.

"The bishop is the spiritual father of the diocese and the sign of unity in the community."

renewal of
baptismal promises

After the homily everyone stands and the bishop invites the Confirmation candidates to reject Satan and to accept the truths of the Catholic Faith. This profession of faith emphasizes the link between Baptism and Confirmation.

You will be renewing the same promises that your parents and godparents made on your behalf when you were baptized. This will probably be the first time that you will be asked publicly to state that you believe in Jesus Christ. It is an important moment. The bishop will expect a confident and audible response to his questions. Make sure that you speak up clearly so that the whole community can hear your profession of faith. You will be answering up together, so there is no need to be nervous.

Baptismal Promises

Bishop: Do you reject Satan and all his works and all his empty promises?

Candidates: I do.

Bishop: Do you believe in God the Father Almighty, Creator of heaven and earth?

Candidates: I do.

Bishop: Do you believe in Jesus Christ,
His only Son, Our Lord,
who was born of the Virgin Mary,
was crucified, died and was buried,
rose from the dead, and is now seated
at the right hand of the Father?

Candidates: I do.

Bishop: Do you believe in the Holy Spirit,
the Lord, the giver of life,
who came upon the Apostles at Pentecost
and today is given to you sacramentally
in Confirmation?

Candidates: I do.

Bishop: Do you believe in the Holy Catholic Church,
the communion of saints,
the forgiveness of sins,
the resurrection of the body,
and life everlasting?

Candidates: I do.

Bishop: This is our Faith. This is the Faith of the Church.
We are proud to profess it in Christ Jesus Our Lord.

Candidates: Amen.

This is the first opportunity for the candidates to profess in public their faith in Jesus Christ.

the prayer of consecration

The Sacrament of Confirmation

The Prayer of Consecration

Everyone kneels down, and the bishop stands at the front facing the candidates. He prays that Almighty God will send down his Holy Spirit upon them as he did upon the Apostles at Pentecost. He begins with a prayer of consecration:

"My dear friends, in baptism God our Father gave the new birth of eternal life
to his chosen sons and daughters. Let us pray to our Father
that he will pour out the Holy Spirit to strengthen his sons and daughters
with his gifts and anoint them to be more like Christ the Son of God."

The Laying on of Hands and Prayer of Consecration

After a short pause for silent prayer, the bishop, together with the priests stands facing the people and they extend their hands over the candidates. This continues a two thousand year old tradition that began with Saints Peter and Paul. Alternatively, the bishop may leave the sanctuary and lay his hands in silence on each candidate in turn.

It is a very solemn moment. The whole community should join with the bishop in praying that the candidates will be blessed and strengthened by the gift and power of the Holy Spirit. The bishop then continues the Prayer of Consecration with these words:

"All powerful God, Father of our Lord Jesus Christ,
by water and the Holy Spirit
you freed your sons and daughters from sin
and gave them new life.
Send your Holy Spirit upon them
to be their helper and guide.
Give them the spirit of wisdom and understanding,
the spirit of right judgement and courage
the spirit of knowledge and reverence,
Fill them with the spirit of wonder and awe in
your presence.
We ask this through Christ our Lord."

All: Amen.

The Anointing with Chrism

Now the candidates in turn come with their sponsor and kneel or stand in front of the bishop. Your sponsor places his/her right hand on your (right) shoulder and gives the card with your chosen confirmation name to the bishop's assistant. The bishop dips his thumb into the chrism oil, lays his hand on top of your head, and with his thumb makes a small sign of the cross on your forehead saying:

Bishop: Anne/Joseph* Be sealed with
                 the gift of the Holy Spirit.
                 (*your chosen name)

The Sign of Peace

Immediately after the anointing, the bishop places his hand on your shoulder and says:

Bishop: Peace be with you.

Candidates: And also with you.

Congratulations! You have now received the sacrament of Confirmation and are fully initiated into the Catholic community. The bishop may take this opportunity to give you a few words of encouragement. Remember to thank him!

general intercessions
eucharistic prayer
holy communion

those who have helped and supported you together with all who have been involved in preparing the church and the liturgy. His final blessing may be in a solemn form which includes three short prayers in honour of the Blessed Trinity. At the end of these he says:

Bishop:	The Lord be with you.
People:	**And also with you..**
Bishop:	Blessed be the name of the Lord.
People:	**Now and for ever.**
Bishop:	Our help is in the name of the Lord.
People:	**Who made heaven and earth.**
Bishop:	May Almighty God bless you †
	The Father, the Son and the Holy Spirit.
People:	**Amen.**

The General Intercessions

We do not say the Creed because we have already professed our Faith when we renewed our Baptismal Promises. The Mass continues with the Prayers of Intercession (Bidding Prayers); the candidates can be involved in preparing and reading these.

The Preparation of the Gifts and the Eucharistic Prayer

Some parishes take a special collection at this point. This, together with the procession of gifts, provides further opportunity for the Confirmation candidates to be involved in the liturgy. The Eucharistic Prayer which follows is the same as the familiar Sunday liturgy.

Holy Communion

All the candidates for Confirmation should have been attending Mass regularly and receiving Holy Communion. If Communion is to be received under both kinds, any candidates who have not previously received from the chalice should have been instructed how to hold the chalice carefully with both hands.

The Final Prayer and Blessing

After the final prayer, the bishop will congratulate those who have been confirmed. He will thank the catechists and

Time to Celebrate!

After Mass, the parish community will probably gather in the church hall for a few refreshments to celebrate your Confirmation. This is a good opportunity to thank your catechists and maybe to give them a present as a token of your appreciation. But remember that by far the most valuable gift you can give to them and to your parish community is for you to continue coming to Mass and taking part in the activities of the parish. There are plenty of opportunities for you to make a contribution to the spiritual and social life of the parish family. This is where you can give a powerful witness to your love of Our Lord. This is what Confirmation is all about.

The reception of Holy Communion completes our celebration of Confirmation.

your questions
about confirmation

Q) What do the words "Be sealed" mean when the Bishop anoints us with chrism?

A) These words remind us that we have been chosen and marked by the Holy Spirit. We are clothed with power to witness to Christ.

The word *seal* combines two ideas:

First, it is a mark of ownership - we now belong to Christ. Second, it is a call to action - we are enrolled in the service of Our Lord. *(Catechism of the Catholic Church 1295.)*

The use of a seal and the ideas behind it are very ancient indeed. A seal is a sign of a person's ownership and authority. Nowadays it would be our signature or our secret pin number for our credit card. In Roman times, soldiers or slaves could be marked with the seal of their owners or legion officer. In medieval times (c1000-1400) legal documents and important letters would be 'sealed' with their owner's signet ring, pressed into melted wax over the opening. This guaranteed the document's authenticity and importance. We still 'seal' an envelope to secure the contents, and some legal documents are secured with a red wax seal, stamped with the firm's badge or logo. Most parishes have an official stamp which is used on official copies of parish records of baptism or marriage.

Q) Why are we anointed with oil at Confirmation?

A) The bishop uses oil because it is the sacramental sign of Confirmation. Each sacrament has an external sign or signs that remind us of the *effect* of the sacrament we are receiving. Scented oil is used in Confirmation to remind us that the Holy Spirit is with us and gives us the spiritual courage to witness to Jesus Christ every day. It is a sign of our union with Jesus Christ and of the protection we receive in this sacrament.

Q) What is so special about oil?
Why is it used so often in the sacraments?

A) Oil is obtained from a variety of sources and is so much a part of our daily lives that we take it for granted. It is used for fuel, to generate electricity, as a lubricant in industry and the home, in plastics, fertilizers, cooking, medicines and cosmetics.

The versatility of oil has been appreciated for thousands of years. Apart from its use in lamps and for cooking it has been highly valued for its many other properties. For example, it cleans and refreshes the body after bathing, and makes it supple and strong for sport. In medicines it heals and soothes sprains and bruises; in cosmetics it softens the skin. It is because of these properties that oil

is used in four of the sacraments. It is used to remind us that, just as the scented oil protects and beautifies the body, so the sacraments, by the power of the Holy Spirit, give us spiritual healing and strength and protect us against evil.

The use of oil in the sacraments is also linked to the Old Testament tradition where people were anointed with oil when they were set apart for the service of God. The most important of these was when they were consecrated as priests or invested with power, authority and responsibility as kings. In 1 Samuel 10.1 we read of Saul being anointed as the first king of God's chosen people by the Judge Samuel. The coronation service at Westminster Abbey contains the religious rite of anointing the monarch's head with oil as a sign of dedication to the service of God and of the people of Britain.

So, when we are anointed at Baptism and Confirmation, we are reminded that we all share in the priesthood of Christ in our own way.

Q) What kind of oil is used?

A) The oil used in Confirmation is called chrism (from the Greek word for *anointing*). This is ordinary olive oil to which a perfume has been added which is an extract of conifer resin called balm or balsam. The bishop blesses this oil at the Chrism Mass on Holy Thursday morning. The same oil is used for Baptism and for the Ordination of priests and bishops. At the Holy Thursday Chrism Mass, two further containers of oil are also blessed by the bishop and clergy. One is used in the sacrament of Anointing of the Sick and the other in Baptism; this is called the Oil of Catechumens.

Q) Why does the bishop make the sign of the cross on the candidate's forehead?

A) The bishop traces the cross on our forehead to remind us that we are able to receive the Holy Spirit at Confirmation only because Jesus Christ suffered and died on the cross for us.

Q) Why does the bishop place his hand on the candidates' heads as he anoints their foreheads with chrism?

A) In the Acts of Apostles we read that the Holy Spirit came down upon people when the Apostles laid hands on them. Nowadays, the bishop lays his hand on the head at the same time as he anoints the sign of the cross on the foreheads with chrism.

The anointing at Baptism and Confirmation reminds us that we all share in the priesthood of Christ. **27**

your questions
about confirmation

Q) Why does the bishop wear a different uniform?

A) The purpose of any uniform is to identify the office or job and not the individual who is exercising it.

Many people wear a uniform at work. The armed services, police, firemen, nurses, supermarket staff-all have their own uniforms; that is why we are unlikely to confuse the traffic warden with the school lollipop lady. The special clothes worn by the clergy at Mass are called *vestments*. They set him apart as representing Our Lord. They have developed over many centuries and most of them have a particular meaning or purpose. The bishop uses extra vestments to those worn by the priest. They are called 'insignia'.

The Pectoral Cross: (from the Latin for *breast*) This is a cross on a chain or cord worn around the neck. The cross is the main symbol of our Faith.

The Ring: The ring symbolizes life-long fidelity in marriage. The bishop's ring on his right hand symbolizes his commitment to care for his people.

The Crozier: This is a staff, curved at the top like a shepherd's crook. It symbolizes the bishop's duty to care for his people as a shepherd cares for his sheep.

The Zucchetto: This is a round purple skullcap worn by the bishop beneath his mitre. In the 6th century it covered the shaved ('tonsured') heads of the clergy. The pope's zucchetto is white and a cardinal's is red.

The Mitre: This is a two - pointed hat with two short bands hanging at the back. It developed from a simple cloth hat. Now it is a sign of God's protection - like a soldier's helmet.

The Pallium: Worn only by archbishops who receive it from the pope as a sign that they share in his authority; it is worn over the chasuble. It is a circular band of white woollen cloth with two hanging pieces at front and back, decorated with six crosses held in place by large pins.

Q) Does Confirmation always have to be given by the bishop?

A) The bishop is the usual (called 'ordinary') minister of this sacrament; but priests can confirm in three particular situations:

1) The bishop may ask priests to help if there is a large number for Confirmation; or he may delegate a priest to administer the sacrament if he is unable to attend himself.

2) When a priest, with permission from the bishop, baptizes and confirms an adult at the Easter Vigil Liturgy on Holy Saturday night.

3) When a priest receives someone into the Church - with Baptism and Confirmation - who is very ill and not expected to survive. This sometimes takes place in hospital.

Q) Why does the bishop adminster Confirmation if the other priests can confirm as well?

A) When we are confirmed we become full members of the Christian community. This is a special time for the candidates and for the parish. The bishop is the spiritual father of the diocese and the sign of unity in the community. One of his duties is to support us in our faith; he visits each parish regularly to give the sacrament of Confirmation, to meet us and encourage us to be faithful to the Gospel.

Q) How often can I be confirmed?

A) The sacraments of Baptism, Confirmation and Holy Orders may be received only once. Our relationship with Our Lord and the Church changes completely and for ever when we receive these sacraments, so there is no need to repeat them.

Q) What is this special relationship?

A) These three sacraments have a spiritual effect on us through the power of the Holy Spirit. This indelible spiritual mark or imprint on our soul is called a *sacramental character*. It begins a relationship with Almighty God that is expressed by the words of the bishop when we are confirmed: "Be sealed with the gift of the Holy Spirit".

a) In Baptism we are reborn into the family of God and share in the life of the risen Lord.

b) In Confirmation we reaffirm this commitment and we receive the gift of the Holy Spirit to strengthen so that we can witness to our Lord.

c) In Holy Orders (the sacrament that ordains men to be a deacon or priest) we are dedicated to the service of God and his people.

Q) Why cannot the bishop or priests get married?

A) Priests, bishops, nuns, monks, and some other members of religious groups, do not marry. When they make their commitment to serve God in the priesthood or religious life, they make a solemn promise (sometimes called a vow) not to share their life with another. The reason for this is that they wish to give their whole life to the service of God and of those committed to their care.

Some people say that unmarried priests and religious men and women are selfish, or even somehow abnormal, and that their way of life is unnatural. The answer is that such a way of life is not *UN*natural; it is *SUPER*natural

We must recognize first of all that no one is obliged to get married. Some people make a deliberate choice not to do so. Others would like to marry and have a family but have not found the right partner. Others may be attracted to their own sex. When men enter the priesthood they accept the Church's discipline of a celibate, unmarried life, dedicated to the service of God; they accept it as a SUPERnatural way of life rather than natural.

This life is the beginning of eternal life with God in heaven. When clergy and religious live a celibate life, it is not because they are against marriage. Far from it. To be able to lead this way of life is a gift from God. It is another example of the many varied gifts of the Holy Spirit. It is called a vocation.

Confirmation continues the work that begins at Baptism.

3rd Sacrament of Initiation (CCC 1322-1419)

The Mass is the sacrifice of Calvary made present for us on the altar. In this section we discover a little more about the idea of sacrifice. Any offering we make to God in love and adoration is a sacrifice.

The Sacrifice of the Mass

"The Holy Mass is the sacrifice of the Body and Blood of Jesus Christ, really present on the altar under the appearances of bread and wine and offered to God for the living and the dead." (Catechism of Christian Doctrine Q 227)

"Say it with flowers!" Why do we offer sacrifice?

We are social beings. We need each other in order to become mature and well - balanced people. Our instinct to show appreciation or sympathy reflects the goodness that is within us. So we give flowers or cards on birthdays, wedding anniversaries and funerals; or we give a quick 'phone call.

A present is a symbol of love. We may give it as a 'peace' offering to say 'sorry' or 'thank you' to someone. We may go to considerable time and trouble to find a suitable gift for someone we love. A present is a kind of sacrifice. Sacrifice and love go together. Love is the reason for sacrifice:

"No one has greater love than this, to lay down one's life for one's friends." (John 15.13)

Sacrifice in Old Testament Times

God required his chosen people to worship him by offering sacrifice. This reflects a deep need felt within human nature to acknowledge a divine power or spirit beyond our human existence, yet at the same time very much part of our lives. Whereas pagan sacrifices were offered to 'feed' their gods and keep them happy, the God of Abraham, Isaac and Jacob did not need anything. He is the creator and provider for his people. The sacrifices offered by the Jews had one thing in common - they were intended to establish, restore or maintain communion (between man and God and man and his fellows). The sacrifice of animals was at the centre of their whole system and the key element here was how the sacrificial blood was used:

"For the life of the flesh is in the blood; and I have given it to you for making atonement for your lives on the altar; for, as life, it is the blood that makes atonement."
(Leviticus 17.11)

The Israelite Sacrifices

Once the Israelites had settled in the promised land, they became farmers, growing cereal crops, vines, olives, vegetables and fruit. Their animals were too precious to be slaughtered just for meat. Cattle, sheep and goats were reared mainly for their milk, wool and hides; and some cattle would be used to draw carts or ploughs. Animals would be slaughtered only for very special occasions, such as a family wedding or religious festivals like Passover. Only the very best farm produce from flock or herd, of grain, bread, wine or oil could be offered in sacrifice to God.

Sin and Peace Offerings

Different sacrifices were offered on different occasions. The sacrifice represented the person who was making the offering. In the case of a sin offering, the pouring out of the animal's blood represented the life of the sinner who deserved to die but who was redeemed by the blood of the sacrificed animal. Peace offerings on the other hand were happier celebrations. The food was first offered to God and then eaten by the worshippers at God's 'invitation'. This was seen as a sign that they now enjoyed the friendship of Almighty God.

What is a Sacrifice?
"A sacrifice is the offering of a victim by a priest to God alone, in testimony of his being the Sovereign Lord of all things." (Catechism of Christian Doctrine Q 275)

The Sacrifice of Isaac
God promised to make Abraham the father of a great nation. Twenty-five years later Abraham and Sara had a son in their old age. Then God put Abraham's faith and obedience to the test when he asked him to sacrifice his only son. (Genesis 22). Abraham was even prepared to do this but an angel of the Lord intervened at the last minute to save the boy's life. A ram was sacrificed instead of Isaac and Abraham named the place God will provide. Abraham showed complete faith, trust and obedience to God throughout his life. His memory is honoured in the first Eucharistic Prayer with the title "our father in faith".

The Church teaches
"The Eucharist is the heart and summit of the Church's life, for in it Christ associates his Church and all her members with his sacrifice of praise and thanksgiving offered once for all on the cross to his Father; by this sacrifice he pours out the graces of salvation on his Body which is the Church." (Catechism of the Catholic Church 14407)

"The sacrifice of the Mass is offered for four ends: first, to give supreme honour and glory to God; secondly, to thank him for all his benefits; thirdly, to satisfy God for our sins and to obtain the grace of repentance; fourthly, to obtain other graces and blessings through Jesus Christ." (Catechism of Christian Doctrine Q 279)

God calls us to holiness

The Mass is the sacrifice of the new and everlasting covenant.

In this section we discover more about the covenant.

What is a Covenant?

A covenant is an agreement between two parties for their mutual benefit. It was often made at the end of a military conflict when a conquering nation would impose a treaty on a defeated people and remind them how fortunate they were. Strict terms would be laid down which they would be obliged to accept in return for protection. Sometimes an animal would be killed and shared (sacrificed) to clinch the deal.

About 1,500 B.C. the Israelites, in common with other peoples, would make these defence treaties with their neighbours.

God makes Covenants with his chosen people

Covenants are mentioned frequently in the Old Testament; marriage contracts, commercial agreements or solemn commitments to serve God. The books of Genesis and Exodus contain several important covenants. For example, when God called Abram away from his country and the rest of his family he promised to make him the father of a great nation:

"I am God Almighty; walk before me and be blameless. And I will make my covenant between me and you and will make you exceedingly numerous ... And I will give to you and to your offspring all the land of Canaan" (Genesis 17.2,8)

The Covenant of Sinai - a Call to Holiness of Life

Some five hundred years after his covenant with Abraham, God entered into a special covenant with his chosen people. It began when he called Moses to liberate the Israelites from slavery in Egypt. God gave Moses a new covenant on Mount Sinai. The Ten Commandments underlined the unique nature of this covenant:

This covenant was a religious call to holiness of life.

- There is only one God. No other worship of a pagan shrine is tolerated.
- God takes the initiative with his loving concern and protection.
- God lays down strict moral laws governing every aspect of human behaviour.

- God lays down strict rules of religious ritual - sabbath rest, temple worship, sacrifice, circumcision.
- God is concerned for the underprivileged, the slaves, strangers, women and orphans.

A new covenant is promised

During the long and turbulent history of God's people, the Sinai covenant was broken and renewed. Through the prophet Jeremiah (31.31) God promised a new covenant:

"Behold the days are coming, says the Lord, when I will make a **new covenant** with the house of Israel and the house of Judah ... I will put my law within them, and I will write it upon their heart; and I will be their God and they shall be my people."

Jesus gives us the New Covenant in his blood at the Last Supper

"Then he took a loaf of bread, and when he had given thanks he broke it and gave it to them saying, 'This is my body which is given for you. Do this in remembrance of me.' And he did the same with the cup after supper, saying, 'This cup that is poured out for you is the **new Covenant** in my blood,'" (Luke 22.19 - 20)

Jeremiah's promise was fulfilled for us when Jesus completed this covenant sacrifice on Calvary, and offered his life in atonement for our sins. The earlier covenant of Sinai has now been completed and perfectly fulfilled by the covenant of Calvary. The sacrificed, Passover lamb of the old covenant is replaced by the sacrificed Lamb of the new and eternal covenant, Jesus Christ, Son of the living God, really present on the altar at Mass.

"This cup that is poured out for you is the new Covenant in my blood." (Luke 22.20)

the mass is the new passover

The Last Supper took place during a celebration of the Jewish Passover feast. In this section we discover more about the wonderful feast of Passover.

Passover and the Last Supper

All four Gospels record Jesus' last supper, and all of them link it both with Jesus' death and with Jewish Passover. Saint John even suggests that Jesus himself was the true Passover Lamb, for, in 19.14 - 17 he says that Jesus was given over to be sacrificed on Passover preparation day (when, as we know, the lambs were being sacrificed in the temple). Saint Paul had already said as much when he told the Corinthians: 'Christ, our Passover Lamb, has been sacrificed'. (1 Corinthians 5.7)

The Feasts of Passover and Unleavened Bread

Passover is the most important Jewish festival. It is also one of the earliest. It began as a spring family festival to ask God's blessing on herds and flocks. It was celebrated on the night of the spring full moon and eaten in haste - possibly a relic of the time when the Jews were still a nomadic people. A choice male kid or lamb was sacrificed and eaten and its blood smeared on doorways to ask God's protection. When Moses led the Jews out of Egypt, in about 1,300 B.C, it was at the time of this Passover celebration; so the feast then took on an even deeper significance. God had passed over and spared the homes that were marked with the blood of the lamb and they had passed from slavery in Egypt to freedom as God's chosen people. Later, the feast also commemorated the giving of the Jewish Law to Moses on Mount Sinai.

The feast became a MEMORIAL SACRIFICE. This means that when they celebrated Passover the Jews considered themselves actually to be present in some mystical way at the original event when God's people were liberated from slavery. The festival was a sign that the Jews accepted God's Covenant with his chosen people.

A separate spring festival, the Feast of Unleavened Bread, was celebrated just before Passover. This also gave thanks to God and asked for his blessing and protection on the first fruits of the harvest. The old yeast was thrown out and the unleavened bread and first fruits were offered to God as part of the spring celebration of new life.

By the time of Our Lord, both these feasts had merged, and Passover developed into an eight - day festival that celebrated the birth of the Jewish people as an independent nation. It began on the first night - the *Seder* or 'service' night - with a special meal for the whole family, during which the story was told of the Exodus from Egypt. No yeast was eaten during Passover; only *matzos* - flat slices of crisp, unleavened bread. The reason given was that the hurried escape from Egypt allowed no time for the bread to rise.

An outline of the Passover meal - the Last Supper

It is generally accepted that Jesus chose the Passover meal for the Last Supper with his disciples. The traditional format opened with the solemn lighting of two candles. The head of the household, holding the first cup of wine, blessed and thanked God for his goodness. This "grace before meals" is mirrored in the opening prayers of offering at Mass: 'Blessed are you, Lord, God of all creation ...' The first of four cups of wine was drunk. Red wine symbolised rejoicing and featured in all the major festivals.

The youngest boy present then asked four traditional questions - about the meal, the Passover lamb, the unleavened bread and the bitter herbs. In reply, the host would read from the *Haggadah* (the 'telling'). This included the Exodus account of the escape from Egypt. Everyone then sang psalms 113 and 114 - called the small *Hallel* ('praise') after which the second cup of wine was drunk.

Next, horse-radish and other bitter herbs were dipped in sweet sauce, charoseth, made from nuts, apples and wine. This was a reminder of the sufferings of the Jews in Egypt. The host would pass it to each person at table, beginning with the special guests. This could have been the sign that Jesus gave to John when he passed the food to Judas. (John 13.26)

The men washed their hands ready for dinner. This would have been a suitable opportunity for Jesus to wash the feet of his disciples. (John 13.3 - 5) The main course was roast lamb, now eaten at leisure, in contrast to the hurried meal that was eaten on the night the Jews escaped from Egypt.

Finally the host blessed the *Matzos* bread and passed a piece to each guest. Jesus could have consecrated the bread at this point. A third cup of blessing was drunk, which Jesus may have consecrated. After singing psalm 136, the *Great Hallel*, the meal ended with the fourth cup of wine and closing prayers. Jesus then left for Gethsemane with Peter, James and John to prepare for his final ordeal. (Since the destruction of Jerusalem in A.D. 70, the Passover meal has altered over the years. It no longer need include roast lamb; and burned egg is added in memory of the destruction of the city and temple.)

"Christ, our Passover Lamb, has been sacrificed." (1 Corinthians 5.7.)

the sacrifice of the mass

(CCC 1322 - 1419)

"The Eucharist is the heart and summit of the Church's life." (CCC1407)

In this section we consider each part of the Mass, the better to appreciate its riches.

Let us Pray

Heavenly Father, your Divine Son
shares his risen life with us in the sacraments.
May your Holy Spirit keep us faithful
to the mystery of his death and resurrection,
and help us always to approach the sacrifice of the Mass
with deep faith, reverence and love.
We ask this through Christ Our Lord. Amen.

We arrive at Church

In many countries Catholics do not have clergy to offer Mass, minister to the sick and dying or forgive sins in the name of Christ. Many suffer discrimination and persecution on account of their faith.

Whenever family pressures allow, we should try to arrive at church in sufficient time to prepare our minds and hearts for Mass. We bring to the Lord our hopes and joys, our fears and failures, our anxieties and our grief. We know that we shall receive healing and strength to take up our cross in the coming week. We are unique creations of a loving God, bought by the blood of the Lamb, with heaven as our destiny.

Genuflection

Religious piety is expressed in various ways; in some cultures a simple bow is the accepted sign of reverence for the Blessed Sacrament. In this country it is still customary to genuflect. Unless prevented by age or infirmity, the right knee should touch the ground next to the left foot, while remaining upright. Sadly, this is often reduced to a quick bob in the general direction of the altar.

The genuflection as a sign of respect and prayer has a long history. In Gethsemane, Jesus knelt to pray to his heavenly Father; grateful disciples knelt in worship of Christ and, later, soldiers knelt before him in mockery. Prisoners of war are often forced to their knees as a sign of submission or humiliation. Apart from romantically inclined suitors who may kneel to propose marriage, people traditionally kneel to receive honours and decorations from the monarch.

Why do we go to Mass?

Since the time of the apostles, Christians have believed that the Mass makes present for us the sacrifice of Jesus Christ, the incarnate Son of God, offered in atonement for the sins of the world, on the cross of Calvary. We believe that at the Last Supper when Jesus said "Do this in memory of me," he wanted us all to meet together in faith and love and to make present his Calvary sacrifice under the appearances of bread and wine. This is what we do every time we come to Mass. This is the Faith of our fathers.

It is an immense privilege to be able to worship God in freedom and even to be in your local church, a sacred place - the house of God and the gate of heaven. The Mass is the most perfect act of worship that we can offer to Almighty God. At every Mass, the sacrifice of Christ's Body and Blood is offered for the living and the dead, no matter how few people may attend or however humble the location or however inadequate the celebrant.

A worthy Celebration

Everything connected with our worship must be the very best we can manage and afford. The priest wears special vestments to preside over the liturgy; he is Christ's representative, our link between God and his people. The servers too, the Ministers of the Word and Extraordinary Ministers of the Eucharist, any instrumentalists, singers and vergers, catechists and welcomers - all have their specific role to play, and should approach their responsibilities with due preparation. Similarly, the vestments, sacred vessels, wine and altar breads, lectionaries and missal - all are dedicated to the service and glory of God and should be treated with reverence and care.

The sign of the Cross with Holy Water

The sign of the cross is probably the earliest prayer that we learn as a child and should be made with care. We dip our right fingers into the holy water and make the sign of the cross by touching our forehead, chest, left then right shoulder before joining our hands. At the same time we say, "In the name of the Father and of the Son and of the Holy Spirit. Amen." We are making a profession of faith in the three Divine Persons of the Blessed Trinity.

The cross is the sign of our salvation. Jesus Christ, the Son of God, died on the cross to take away our sins, reconciling us to our heavenly Father. The holy water also reminds us of our Baptism which cleanses us of sin and brings us into the family of God. We are anointed with his Spirit and share in his divine life of sanctifying grace; and we are called to witness to him every day.

the penitential rite
the liturgy of the word

The Mass begins

The priest and servers process from the sacristy through the church to the sanctuary. If possible the procession will be led by a thurifer with the thurible of burning incense, followed by a cross bearer and two acolytes with lighted candles. During the procession the people sing a hymn or gathering song appropriate to the season or solemnity. When they reach the sanctuary, the priest and the servers genuflect to the Blessed Sacrament; otherwise they will bow to the altar.

The priest then kisses the altar because it is a symbol, a reminder of the presence of Our Lord among us. The altar is the rock where the sacrifice of Calvary is made present. It is the table of the Last Supper from which Christ will feed us in Holy Communion. The altar also represents the whole Church and for this reason it contains relics of the saints and martyrs who have lived and died for their Faith. If there is incense, the priest will use it to reverence the altar.

The Penitential Rite

The priest may first welcome us and give a brief introduction to the celebration; and the liturgy begins with the sign of the cross together and the priest's greeting. He begins with the Penitential Rite in which we all, priest and people, acknowledge our sins and ask for forgiveness and healing.

On Sundays during the year and on feasts and solemnities, we say or sing the "Glory to God .." This hymn of praise begins with the words attributed to the angels at the birth of the child Jesus. (Luke 2.14) The priest invites us to pray, and, after a few moments for silent prayer, he gathers our thoughts into an opening prayer called the Collect. This same prayer is said wherever Mass is celebrated throughout the world; it is offered for the whole Church and is addressed to God the Father through Jesus Christ Our Lord.

The Liturgy of the Word

The scripture readings are planned so that we can become familiar with the most important scripture texts over the course of a three year Sunday cycle and a two - year weekly cycle. The first two readings and the responsorial psalm are usually read by one of the parish Ministers of the Word. The first reading is taken from the Old Testament and is linked to the theme of the Gospel. God's message was first revealed in the books of the Old Testament. This is followed by the responsorial psalm and the second reading from one of the New Testament books other than the Gospels. These contain profound spiritual messages as well as practical advice and encouragement. After this reading we stand and greet the Gospel by singing the Alleluia ("Praise God").

The Gospel

The Gospel is read by the priest or a deacon. Candles and incense should be carried if available. The Gospels are no less profound and challenging than the other scripture texts but they are generally more familiar to us and may be easier to understand. They contain the teachings of Jesus, descriptions of events, miracles and parables. As with the other books of the Bible, we still need to appreciate the depths of their message. That is why we have the homily.

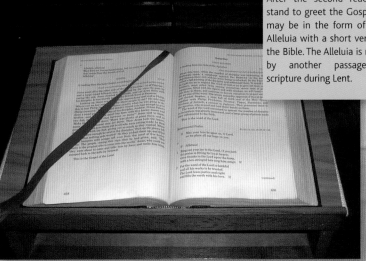

Reverence in church

There is often a lively hubbub in many churches before Mass. It is good to be full of joy in our Faith, but we should also show reverence for the Real Presence of Our Lord in the tabernacle. At the same time we should be mindful of those who have come to church early in order to seek a time for quiet prayer before Mass begins. God speaks to us most often in the quiet of our hearts. We should aim to talk to God before Mass and to each other afterwards, preferably outside or in the entrance area.

First Reading and Psalm

The responsorial psalm is our prayerful response to the first reading we have heard. The psalms are religious songs and should be sung whenever possible. Even when recited they should never be rushed; they are prayers in poetry. They sum up the yearnings of the human heart, searching for God. Jesus would have learned some of them from Mary and sung them in the synagogue.

Second Reading and Gospel Greeting

After the second reading we stand to greet the Gospel. This may be in the form of a sung Alleluia with a short verse from the Bible. The Alleluia is replaced by another passage from scripture during Lent.

the homily

the creed
the prayer of the faithful

The Christian Bible contains two sections - the Old Testament and the New Testament. The Old Testament is a collection of about forty books, written over a period of a thousand years and divided by Hebrew scholars into three main groups-the Law, the Prophets and the Writings. There are many different literary styles - lists of laws and commandments, popular religious stories, historical accounts and records, religious songs and poems, wise sayings, proverbs and prophecies. The New Testament contains the four Gospels, Acts of Apostles and twenty - one letters from the apostles. The Hebrew bible contains only the Old Testament writings.

The "Prayer of the Faithful"
In the early Church, only the fully initiated members of the Christian community were allowed to remain for the whole of Mass; and for this reason the central act of worship, the Eucharistic Prayer with the words of Consecration followed by the reception of Holy Communion, was called the *Mass of the Faithful*. The bidding prayers formed part of the *Mass of the Faithful*.
The *Catechumens*, those who were under instruction in preparation for their baptism at the Easter Vigil, were allowed to stay only for the first part of the Mass - the Liturgy of the Word - so that they could listen to the Gospel and receive instruction in the homily. This part of the Mass became known as the *Mass of the Catechumens*.
In parts of the U.K. the hierarchy has supported the custom of adding a final prayer to Our Blessed Lady, usually the Hail Mary. Mary is the Mother of the Church and it is fitting that she should lead us in our prayer to our heavenly Father. In the Middle Ages, devotion to Our Lady was so popular in England that the country became known as "the dowry of Mary."

The homily

When we listen to the scriptures being read at Mass, Our Lord becomes present to us in his Word. This has been described as a kind of consecration - just as Jesus becomes present sacramentally on the altar when the priest speaks the words of consecration. Then, when the priest explains the Gospels to us in the homily, we receive Christ into our hearts; and this has been likened to a spiritual communion.

The priest is ordained to offer the sacrifice of the Mass, to forgive sin and to preach the Gospel. The homily is thus an essential part of his ministerial responsibilities. A good homily or sermon opens our hearts to God and enriches our faith. It will usually be based on the Gospel that we have just heard and it may explain a point of doctrine, give spiritual guidance or encourage us in our daily lives. It should feed our hunger for God. Ideally, the homily should aim to touch as many as possible in the worshipping community. The homily should not be boring, too long or too academic. It should avoid becoming over emotional, trivial or frivolous. It is not easy to preach a good homily.

The Creed

The Nicene Creed which we now say or sing is a summary of Christian doctrine. It is based on an earlier profession of faith which we know as the *Apostles Creed*, because it dates from the time of the Apostles. When we say or sing the Creed together as a local parish community, we should try to remember that we are united with our brothers and sisters throughout the world,

proclaiming the same Catholic faith that has been taught by the Church since the time of Christ, over two thousand years ago. We may quickly become familiar with the words of this great profession of faith and praise of God, but it takes a lifetime, here and hereafter, to begin to appreciate the profound mystery of God's love for us.

The Prayer of the Faithful

We remain standing for this closing part of the Liturgy of the Word. The Prayer of the faithful (also known as the *Prayers of Intercession* or simply the *Bidding Prayers*) is a list of intercessions that are offered for the needs of the universal Church and the world, as well as for the national and local communities. These will include the sick and dying of the parish, those who are to be baptised or who are preparing to receive the other sacraments and other special intentions of the local parish community.

The priest introduces the intercessions with an opening prayer and one of the community then announces each intention. After a short pause for silent prayer, we say or sing a response, e.g. "Lord, in your mercy: Hear our prayer."

"The Creed is the people's response to the word of God in the readings, explained in the homily.

the preparation of the gifts

The Liturgy of the Eucharist

In the first part of the Mass, we meet Our Lord in his spoken Word. The priest speaks to the people *on behalf of God*, as his representative, explaining some of the profound truths of our faith. This prepares us for the central act of worship, the Sacrifice of the Mass in which we meet Our Lord in the Liturgy of the Eucharist. Here the priest will be speaking to God, interceding *on behalf of the people*.

The focus of our attention now shifts from the lectern (also called the ambo or pulpit) to the altar. The first part of the Mass, the Liturgy of the Word, can be led by a lay person, for example when a Eucharistic Service is held in the absence of a priest. The central act of our worship requires the presence of a bishop or a priest.

The Preparation of the Gifts

We all sit down while the collection is being taken and the servers prepare the altar. A square piece of white cloth (called the *corporal*) is placed in the centre of the altar, with the missal to one side and the chalice, purificator cloth and paten for the large altar bread, on the other. During this time there may be an offertory hymn, some quiet organ music or a motet from the choir. These relatively quiet moments give us the opportunity to reflect that we are shortly to be offering, through the priest, the sacrifice of Jesus Christ to his heavenly Father.

The gifts brought to the altar in procession are for the sacrifice of the Mass or the service of the church and the poor. They remind us all that this is *our* sacrifice. We are offering ourselves in worship and adoration of Almighty God. In return, God will give himself to us in Holy Communion. (Any other tokens of our daily life and work should be placed on the sanctuary before Mass begins).

Why does the priest add water to the wine?

After the celebrant has received the gifts at the altar steps, he goes to the altar, holds the ciborium containing the altar breads and says a prayer of thanksgiving and blessing. During the time of Christ it was customary to dilute the wine at table. The priest then pours wine into the chalice(s) and adds a few drops of water while quietly saying a short prayer which

goes to the heart of the Eucharist. "By the mystery of this water and wine, may we come to share in the divinity of Christ, who humbled himself to share in our humanity." In this prayer we ask that we may be as closely united with Our Lord in Holy Communion as the water that merges completely with the wine in the chalice. The gifts, the priest and the people may then be incensed as a sign of respect.

The priest washes his hands

The priest now moves to the side of the altar where a server with water and a towel assists him to rinse his hands. This could be necessary after handling the gifts and the thurible, but it also has a religious symbolism that reaches back to early Christianity and Judaism. While washing his hands he says; "Lord, wash away my iniquity. Cleanse me from my sins." The priest is a sinner before God, so he prays to be purified and cleansed from sin as he prepares to offer the Eucharistic Sacrifice.

Returning to the centre of the altar he addresses the people: "Pray, brethren, that my sacrifice and yours may be acceptable to God the almighty Father." The people acknowledge that the priest is offering the sacrifice on their behalf: "May the Lord accept the sacrifice at your hands, for the praise and glory of his name, for our good and the good of all his Church."

The Prayer over the Offerings

This part of the Liturgy draws to a close with a short prayer said by the priest over the offerings. Like the opening prayer of the Mass, it draws together all our prayers and thoughts before we begin the central act of sacrificial worship in the Eucharistic Prayer.

"The procession with the gifts expresses the assembly's participation in the Eucharist."

The Preface and "Holy, holy"

The central part of the Mass opens with the Preface prayer. The priest gives thanks and praise to God the Father through Jesus Christ on behalf of us all. The prayer highlights the religious season or solemnity and ends by thanking and praising God in company with the angels and saints. It leads into a response which we all say or sing, also called the Sanctus (Latin for *Holy*): "Holy, holy, holy Lord, God of power and might, heaven and earth are full of your glory. Hosannah in the highest. Blessed is he who comes in the name of the Lord. Hosannah in the highest."

Holy, Holy, Holy.
The first part of this acclamation is taken from the prophecy of Isaiah (6.1) where he describes his vision of angels worshipping God in heaven. The second part is taken from the Passion (Palm) Sunday Gospel reading. Saint Matthew (21.9) describes the Jerusalem children welcoming Jesus as he enters the city riding on a donkey.

The Eucharistic Prayer
In the earliest days of Christianity, the priest would probably improvise prayers of praise and thanksgiving. These would very likely be based on some of the Jewish prayers which the early Christian converts would have known from their childhood. He would then say the words of consecration over the bread and wine. As time passed the text began to be written down, although it would vary from place to place.
By the seventh century, there was only one official text used in the western Church. This was known as the *Roman Canon*; it remained, largely unchanged, for almost fourteen hundred years. In 1969, a further three texts were approved by the Church for general use and others were added later. Despite these additions and variations, they all share the same words of Consecration.

The Eucharistic Prayer

We kneel down for the central act of worship. Each of the four Eucharistic Prayers has the same general outline with six main sections:

1) The calling down of the Holy Spirit (Greek-*Epiclesis*)

The priest holds his hands over the gifts of bread and wine and prays that, through the power of the Holy Spirit, they may become the body and blood of Our Lord. This prayer and the laying on of hands comes near the beginning of the second and third Eucharistic prayers but a little later in the other two.

2) The words of Consecration

When the priest repeats the words and actions of Our Lord, the sacrifice which he gave us at the Last Supper is made present. Jesus offers his body and blood for us under the appearances of bread and wine.

3) The Commemoration (Greek-*Anamnesis*)

The priest reminds us that the words of consecration make the Passion, Death, Resurrection and Ascension of Jesus really present on the altar under the sacramental signs of bread and wine. This is why the Mass is a Memorial Sacrifice. The actual words used vary slightly but their meaning is the same:

1st prayer; "Father, we celebrate the memory of Christ, your Son."

2nd prayer; "In memory of his death and resurrection ..."

3rd prayer; "Calling to mind the death, resurrection and ascension"

4th prayer; "We now celebrate this memorial of our redemption ..."

4) The Offering

The priest, again speaking on our behalf, offers to our heavenly Father the sacrificial victim, Jesus, the Son of God. We can also offer ourselves and our lives in union with Our Lord to almighty God.

5) The Intercessions

Here we are reminded that the Mass is offered throughout time and in every corner of the world for all God's people, living and dead. We remember those who have "fallen asleep in Christ", especially those who are dear to us. We remember our own intentions and bring them to the mercy of God.

6) The final Prayer of Praise

Each Eucharistic Prayer ends as the priest, raising the consecrated bread and wine, says or sings the closing prayer: "Through him, with him, in him, in the unity of the Holy Spirit, all glory and honour is yours almighty Father, for ever and ever." We show our agreement and proclaim our faith in the Real Presence, when we reply "Amen."

"I am the living bread that came down from heaven." (John 6.51)

The Lord's Prayer and Doxology

We prepare for our Holy Communion by standing to say or sing the Our Father. The priest asks that we may be delivered from every evil and anxiety. Our reply is an early Christian doxology: "For the kingdom, the power and the glory are yours, now and forever."

The Rite of Peace

This sign means we really believe we are brothers and sisters in Christ, whose presence we acknowledge in each other. In the early Church it was the custom to exchange a ritual kiss of peace when the Offertory gifts were brought to the altar. Jesus said:

"First be reconciled to your brother or sister and then come and offer your gift." (Matthew 5.24)

The "Lamb of God" prayer

The priest takes the large host and breaks off a small portion which he then places in the chalice containing the Precious Blood. As he does so he says, "May this mingling of the Body and Blood of Our Lord Jesus Christ bring eternal life to us who receive it." While he is doing this, we say or sing the "Lamb of God" prayer. If large hosts are used, the prayer may be repeated until the breaking is completed.

The breaking of the bread

This symbol reminds us that, though many, we are all united in the one Body of Christ. In the early Church a small fragment of consecrated host was reserved after Mass and added to the consecrated chalice at the Mass on the following day. This was a reminder that the same sacrifice of Calvary is made present at each Mass. The same custom was observed in Rome, where a fragment of consecrated host from the Pope's Mass would be carried to another basilica and mingled with the Precious Blood at Mass.

The "Lord, I am not worthy" prayer

The priest pauses to pray silently before he receives Holy Communion. He genuflects, raises the Sacred Host and Chalice and introduces a prayer that includes the words of a Roman centurion who showed great respect for Jesus and immense faith in his power of healing:

"This is the Lamb of God, who takes away the sins of the world. Happy are those who are called to his supper. Lord, I am not worthy to receive you under my roof. Say but the word and my soul shall be healed." (Matthew 8.8.)

We receive Holy Communion

The time of Holy Communion is a precious and sacred climax of the Mass. We are encouraged to receive Holy Communion under both kinds but Our Lord is wholly and entirely present under either or both species of the consecrated bread and wine.

The purifying of vessels and hands

Any remaining Precious Blood is consumed, spare consecrated hosts in the ciborium are returned to the tabernacle, the priest washes his hands and the sacred vessels are cleansed.

The silent prayer of thanksgiving

The *General Instruction on the Roman Missal* (2005 No 88) suggests: "...The priest and the faithful spend some time in praying quietly." In their commentary, Celebrating the Mass (2005 no 215) the English and Welsh bishops add: "When Communion is completed, the whole assembly may observe a period of total silence. In the absence of all words, actions, music or movement, a moment of deep corporate stillness and contemplation may be expressed. Such silence is important to the rhythm of the whole celebration and is welcome in a busy and restless world."

The Blessing and Dismissal

The closing words of the Mass remind us of our calling to witness to Christ every day. God has work for us to do which he has entrusted to no one else. The Holy Spirit gives us power and courage to do God's will. The Mass closes with the final prayer. We give thanks for God's loving mercy and pray that we may grow in love of him. Any announcements can now be made and the priest gives the final blessing and dismisses us with the commission: "The Mass is ended. Go in peace to love and serve the Lord." We reply, "Thanks be to God."

"Whoever eats this bread will live for ever." (John 6.51)

different names given to the eucharist

A note on Transubstantiation

For centuries, Christians struggled to find an adequate description of what happens when the priest says the words of consecration over the bread and wine. How can anyone express the depth of this mystery? In the 13th century, Saint Thomas Aquinas used the term Transubstantiation which the philospher Aristotle (4th century B.C.) had used to describe the difference between the inner reality or substance of something (e.g. our character and personality) and its accidents (e.g. our changing external appearance).

Saint Thomas used this distinction when writing about the consecration at Mass. He said that the *substance* or inner reality of the bread and wine are changed and become the *substance* or inner reality of the Body, Blood, Soul and Divinity of Jesus Christ. The appearances and qualities of the bread and wine, their *accidents*, remain unchanged.

In the 16th century, the Protestant reformers said that Christ did not become present at the Consecration. They denied the doctrine of the Real Presence of Our Lord in the Eucharist. In 1551, the Council of Trent used the term Transubstantiation once again in order to re-state the Catholic teaching on the Eucharist. The presence of Our Lord in the Eucharist is sacramental, not physical; under the outward sign and appearance of bread and wine.

Why purify hands and sacred vessels at Mass?

Hygiene requires that the paten, chalices and ciboria be carefully cleansed after coming into contact with the Blessed Sacrament; they will have been handled by several people. From a religious perspective, the 'purifying' of sacred vessels symbolises our respect and reverence for all things sacred, especially the Blessed Sacrament.

The Jewish law had strict rules about ritual purity and Our Lord respected these. At the same time he also stressed that real purity was not so much about outward and external matters, rather does it lie within our own heart and conscience. (Mark 7.6-23)

The Breaking of Bread

When we make friends with someone, we may invite them round to our place for a meal. It does not have to be anything special, but it is a gesture of friendship and it is a valued social custom in many cultures throughout the world.

In the early Church, the Mass was sometimes called "The Breaking of Bread." At the Last Supper, Jesus broke the bread and gave it to his disciples, as was the custom for the host at a Jewish meal. "While they were eating, he took a loaf of bread, and after blessing it he broke it, gave it to them, and said, 'Take, this is my body.'" (Mark 14.22) The same expression is used when Jesus appeared to the two disciples at Emmaus. (Luke 24.35) and in Acts, "On the first day of the week, when we met to break bread,..." (Acts 20.7)

Holy Communion

This is the term we use for the Body and Blood of Christ we receive at Mass. If there is no priest available to offer Mass on a Sunday, an Extraordinary Minister of Holy Communion may be allowed to lead what is called a *Eucharistic Service*. After the greeting, confession of sins and liturgy of the Word, all say the Our Father and the Minister then distributes Holy Communion from the tabernacle. These Communion services may become more frequent as priests decline in number.

The Holy Eucharist - The Real Presence

The word Eucharist comes from the Greek for *thanksgiving*. At the Last Supper, Jesus consecrated the bread and wine during the Passover prayer of praise and thanksgiving. At Mass, the priest, following the directions of Our Lord, calls down the Holy Spirit upon the bread and wine and asks that they may become the Body and Blood of Christ. When he says the words of consecration, Jesus Christ, the Son of God, becomes really present on the altar.

The Lord's Supper

The only parish Mass that may be celebrated on Holy Thursday is called the *Evening Mass of the Lord's Supper*. This commemorates the Last Supper when Jesus consecrated the bread and wine for the first time and gave himself to us in Holy Communion. At the same gathering he ordained the first priests and gave the new commandment that we should love each other; and washed the feet of his disciples as an example of how we should care for each other.

The Blessed Sacrament

This expression again means the sacramental presence of Our Lord in the consecrated bread and wine. Some Sacred Hosts are always reserved in the tabernacle so that Holy Communion can be taken at any time to the sick or dying. The Blessed Sacrament is available for private devotional visits or public veneration in services of Exposition and Benediction.

Viaticum

This word means *Food for the journey*. It is used of Holy Communion when it is given to someone who is dying. When the three sacraments of Confession, Anointing of the Sick and Holy Communion are given to a dying person they are sometimes referred to as the *Last Sacraments* or even as the *Last Rites*.

"The bread that I will give for the life of the world is my flesh." (John 6.51)

extraordinary ministers of the eucharist

Preparing for Holy Communion

We can never be worthy to receive the gift of Christ himself in Holy Communion. We should prepare for this sacred moment by taking our full part in the celebration of Mass and by our own private prayers of faith, hope and love of God. If we are aware that we have serious sin on our conscience then we should always seek absolution in Confession before Mass. The opportunity for Confession is usually readily available.

When approaching the altar for Holy Communion we should do so with eyes lowered and hands joined. This helps us to be recollected and to focus on the sacred moment that we are about to experience. Modesty in dress is part of reverence. Our respect for the person of Christ, as well as for our brothers and sisters and indeed for ourselves also, should help us to exercise moderation on the vagaries of fashion. This is particularly important for those who exercise the privileged role of Extraordinary Ministers of the Eucharist.

How to receive Holy Communion

Since 1965 there has been a choice of ways in which to receive Holy Communion - on the tongue or in the hand, under the form of bread alone, or of both bread and wine. The earlier tradition of kneeling to receive Communion is now replaced by the present custom of approaching the altar in an orderly queue and remaining standing. No other specific act of reverence is now required.

When receiving Holy Communion in the hand, the receiving hand should be supported by the other so that it forms a cradle. The priest places the Sacred Host in the upper hand while saying "The Body of Christ." We reply "Amen", step to one side and then reverently place the Sacred Host into the mouth with the lower hand. We should not move from this position until the Sacred Host is safe. The priest will not usually place the Sacred Host on a gloved or bandaged hand.

When receiving the Precious Blood, the chalice should be held firmly but gently in both hands. Great care should be taken not to jolt the chalice. The priest or Extraordinary Eucharistic Minister will usually keep hold of the chalice for those with unsteady hands and incline it gently towards the communicant. Consideration for others suggests that we do not receive from the chalice if we have a heavy cold. We receive the whole Christ, body, blood, soul and divinity, under the form either of bread or wine.

Ordinary and Extraordinary Ministers

Ordinary Ministers of the Eucharist are bishops, priests and deacons. Extraordinary Ministers are specially commissioned lay men or women. Their office may be traced back to the practice of the early Church when the Blessed Sacrament would be taken at the end of Mass to those who were sick at home, possibly by ordained deacons. Extraordinary Ministers are usually commissioned, for one year, during the Evening Mass of the Lord's Supper on Holy Thursday. This may be renewed for several successive years.

Extraordinary Ministers should only exercise their office if and when there is a shortage of ordained clergy. While they are usually in evidence at Sunday Masses throughout the country, especially if Holy Communion is received under both kinds, perhaps their most valuable role is in making home visits, often during the week, to the sick and elderly, be they at home, in hospital or in nursing homes.

The Eucharistic Fast

The Church has directed that, as a sign of respect, food and drink may not be taken for one hour before receiving Holy Communion. Water and necessary medicines are allowed. The elderly, the sick and those who care for them are not bound by this regulation. One pious custom, now largely forgotten, was on returning from Mass, always to break one's fast with a drink of water before taking any other nourishment.

Where does the word 'Mass' come from?

One possible answer is that the name Mass comes from the Latin word 'missa' which means *dismissal*. In the early Church, the Catechumens (those who were being instructed before Baptism) were dismissed from the assembly before the most sacred part of the Mass, the Eucharistic Prayer, began.

However, it seems that the most likely explanation for the term *Mass* is that the Mass ends with the 'dismissal' when the priest dismisses us and sends us out to bear witness to our Faith in our daily lives.

"Holy Communion is the shortest and safest way to Heaven." (Pope St Pius X)

vocation ... christian

priesthood   diaconate   religious life

Our Vocation as Christians

The Latin word 'vocare' means to *call*. At our Baptism we become followers of Christ; when we are confirmed we are called to witness to Our Lord every day. This is the vocation of all our baptised and confirmed brothers and sisters throughout the world. For most of us, our path through life will follow the vocation of marriage and parenthood; for others it will be as a single person or maybe in a religious order or as a priest or deacon. Each vocation is important in the sight of God because each of us is gifted differently by the Holy Spirit. The word *vocation* is also used to describe careers that require a life of dedicated service of others, like medicine, nursing or teaching. However, Catholics tend to use the term *vocation* mainly when referring to the priesthood, diaconate or religious life.

Religious Orders

Most religious orders of men or women can be classified as either *Contemplative* or *Active*. Contemplative orders of men or women are so called because their chief work is the worship of God through public liturgy and private prayer. So - called 'enclosed' orders will rarely leave their house, convent or monastery. Some support themselves by making altar breads, vestments, pottery, religious art or craft work or by bookbinding or printing. Others live from day to day, relying on public charity. These communities of men or women quickly become centres for spiritual counselling and bereavement support; they fulfil a vital role in the local community and are valued highly by those who seek their help.

Active or pastoral orders of men or women specialise in a particular apostolate or sphere of work. This could be in teaching, nursing, missionary activities abroad, caring for the elderly and terminally ill, working among the socially marginalized, as parish assistants or catechists, or preaching missions and retreats in parishes and schools. As with any large family, the daily duties are shared by the members of the community, directed by the superior. There is usually a period of about two years of assessment and training (called the novitiate) after which the members make their religious vows.

The Vocation of a Priest?

The Church IS people; it is a worldwide family of believers, the people of God. If a man feels drawn to serve God in the priesthood, he could take the first step of speaking to his parish priest who will put him in touch with the diocesan Director of Vocations. After guidance and assessment he may then begin his studies, usually a period of about six years. This lengthy period allows the candidate to get to know and understand himself better and to develop his own personal relationship with our Lord. He will study the teaching of the Church and the truths of faith, philosophy, the theology of the sacraments, the Church's moral teaching, Church history, canon law and also the important pastoral skills needed in this ministry. He will usually have a parish placement as part of his training.

What does it take to become a Priest?

The main element in discerning if a person has a vocation to the priesthood is the call of the Church. Sincerity, piety and intelligence are not enough. It is God who calls a person to serve in the priesthood through the Church in the person either of the bishop or the leader of a religious order. In assessing the suitability of a possible candidate, the bishop or religious leaders will be looking for someone who is unmarried, in good health, mature, intelligent, persevering, generous and of a stable disposition. The person needs to be a man of prayer, with a strong faith and a desire to serve Almighty God. It would be wrong to seek the priesthood for unworthy or secular motives - for example because it seems to offer a secure job for life, with a house, a reasonable standard of living and the use of a car.

The Vocation of a Deacon

The Greek word 'diakonia' means *service*. Deacons were first commissioned in the early Church to serve the Christian community. Nowadays, with the decline in the number of priests, the permanent deacons fulfil an increasingly important role in the parish community. Deacons can baptise, preach and conduct wedding and funeral services. They may be part of a hospital chaplaincy team and give invaluable help and support in many areas of parish life. The vocation is open to married men. The preparatory studies are spread over several years and involve distance learning and some residential tutorials and retreats.

The Vocation of Religious Life

There are many different religious congregations for men and women, but most will have some things in common. Members will usually live in community; they will often pray, work and eat together and they follow a spiritual 'rule' of life that has been drawn up by their founder or foundress. They make three solemn promises called *vows*. The first of these is *Poverty* - by which they promise to live a simple life, be detached from money and not to own private property. The second is *Chastity* - by which they sacrifice their right to marriage in order to seek and serve God in others. The third is *Obedience* - by which they submit their lives to God's will as directed by their religious superior.

The Wider Vocation of Service in the Community

Other valuable vocations include lay communities of married people on short - term voluntary missionary, medical work or in communities supporting the handicapped or the disposssessed of our inner cities.

"Jesus said to them; 'Follow me and I will make you fish for people.'" (Mark 1.17)

choosing between right and wrong

> **Let us Pray**
>
> *Heavenly Father,*
> *Thank you for our families and friends.*
> *Guide us with your Holy Spirit to choose the*
> *good and always to follow our conscience.*
> *We ask this through Christ Our Lord. Amen.*

We have a sense of Justice

Everybody seems to have an instinctive sense of right and wrong. Lots of arguments at home start if the children think they have been overlooked or treated unfairly. They say "It's not fair!" At a soccer match the crowd will soon let the referee know if they think he has made a wrong decision. We all get annoyed if we have been unjustly accused or treated unjustly.

The Natural Law

This sense of right and wrong is hard-wired into our human nature. Our conscience helps us to make these judgments about good and evil. Our conscience has been given to us by God:

> "Deep within our conscience we discover a law which we must obey ... This law calls us to love good and avoid evil. It is a law written in our heart by God. Our conscience is our secret place where we are alone with God whose voice echoes within us." *(Catechism of the Catholic Church 1776, quoting from the Vatican II document on the Church in the Modern World No. 16.)*

Our Conscience has to be formed

God has given us a sense of right and wrong, and as we grow up our parents gradually fine-tune our conscience to help us make the correct decisions in different situations. Theirs is a serious responsibility. We begin learning when we are still very young. Our parents and teachers show us the right way to think, speak and behave. They correct us when we do something bad, wrong, selfish or dangerous, and give us lots of praise when we are good.

So we learn to be kind and considerate, to tell the truth, to respect each other, to obey our parents and school staff, to forgive and forget. As we grow older our conscience gradually

becomes a reliable guide for our thinking and behaviour and we learn to decide correctly between right and wrong. Sometimes our judgment can be mistaken, so we must always try to find out the truth. If we are not sure, we can ask someone what the Church teaches or check it out for ourselves on a web site.

Three Good Rules

1) We may not do evil so that good may come of it. Good intentions never justify bad actions.

2) We must always follow our conscience. We must always respect another's conscience.

3) "Do to others as you would have them do to you." (Luke 6.31)

   This is called the golden rule; it was given to us by Our Lord himself.

> **The Natural Law**
> The Roman political writer Cicero (106-43 B.C.) said: "For there is a true law: right reason. It is in conformity with nature, is diffused among all men and is immutable and eternal; its orders summon to duty; its prohibitions turn away from offence ... To replace it with a contrary law is a sacrilege; failure to apply even one of its provisions is forbidden; no one can abrogate it entirely." *(Republic III.22,33)*
>
> Not everyone accepts that there is such a thing as a Natural Law; but there is general agreement that human reason does tend to accept certain principles of good behaviour.

free will   grace   sin

The Church Teaches ...

Free Will
"Endowed with a spiritual soul, with intellect and with free will, the human person is from his very conception ordered to God and destined for eternal beatitude. He pursues his perfection in "seeking and loving what is true." *(Catechism of the Catholic Church 1711)*

Grace
"Grace is favour, the free and undeserved help that God gives us to respond to his call to become children of God, adoptive sons, partakers of the divine nature and of eternal life." *(Catechism of the Catholic Church 1996)*

Sin
"Sin is an offence against God, by any thought, word, deed, or omission against the law of God."*(Catechism of Christian Doctrine Q 113)*

"Sin is an act contrary to reason. It wounds man's nature and injures human solidarity...The root of all sins lies in man's heart." *(Catechism of the Catholic Church 1872-1873)*

"To choose deliberately - that is, both knowing it and willing it - something gravely contrary to the divine law and to the ultimate end of man is to commit a mortal sin..." *(Catechism of the Catholic Church 1874)*

Original Sin
The colourful account of the fall of Adam and Eve in the book of Genesis is a figurative description of mankind's rejection of God at the beginning of human history. This sin of pride led us to disobey God. It was a refusal to accept that we are creatures, totally dependent on our Creator. This original rejection of God's love and law has weakened human nature and resulted in a world that is damaged by sin. When we commit sin we are putting our own desires, our own will, before the will and law of God. This damages ourselves because we turn away from what is good and true and choose instead something that we think is better, but which is wrong.
The Devil or Satan is a fallen angel whose power is limited because he is a created spirit. Satan told our first parents that they could disobey God's will. Our Redeemer, Jesus Christ, died on the cross in obedience to his Heavenly Father's will and so atoned for our sin and redeemed us from sin and death.

Free Will

God created each one of us as a unique human being. We are made 'in the image and likeness of God'. This means that we have a spiritual and immortal soul, an independent mind and the freedom to choose truth and goodness - called free will.

God shares his life with us through grace which we receive in the sacraments and through his gifts to us of faith, hope and love. He has given us human reason to seek God. God gives his grace to help us share his divine nature. We have free will so we can choose freely to do right or wrong.

Grace

Grace is God's free gift of life and love within us. Grace is called 'sanctifying' because it helps us grow closer to the holiness of God. We first begin to share in God's life of grace when we are baptised. We are in a 'state of grace' when we are united to God's loving friendship. If we reject God's love by serious sin we lose this 'state of grace'; we regain it when we repent of doing wrong, confess our sins and receive forgiveness (called 'absolution') in the Sacrament of Penance.

Our Lady is "Full of Grace" because she is perfectly united to God's love. She was conceived free from sin. Mary was preserved from original sin so that she could be a fitting mother of our Redeemer. This special grace given to Mary is called the 'Immaculate Conception'.

Making the right choices

Because we have been given free will we can deliberately ignore what our conscience tells us and choose

to do something which is against what God wants for our happiness. This is what happens when we commit sin. Saint John said:

> "If we say that we have no sin, we deceive ourselves, and the truth is not in us. If we confess our sins, he who is faithful and just will forgive our sins and cleanse us from all unrighteousness."
> (1 John 1.8 - 9)

Sin

Sin comes from our heart when we freely choose to do wrong. Sin is an offence against God. It is a failure to love God when we break his commandments. It harms ourselves and other people and it destroys the love that should fill our lives. Jesus showed us that some of our sins are more serious than others:

> "Woe to you, scribes and pharisees, hypocrites! For you ... have neglected the weightier matters of the Law; justice and mercy and faith. It is these you ought to have practised without neglecting the others. You blind guides! You strain out a gnat but swallow a camel!"
> (Matthew 23.23)

"Love your enemies. ... Be merciful just as your Father is merciful." (Luke 6. 35 - 36)

making the right choices

Sin can be grave or less serious

Most of our daily faults and failings - impatience, unkindness, jealousy or anger, are less serious (called 'venial') offences; they do not reject God's love. But, if we were deliberately to break God's law in a serious matter, then we can be in a state of grave (or 'mortal') sin. Three conditions would have to be present before we could commit a mortal sin:

Grave matter: Serious sins would be things like murder, abortion, or being unfaithful in marriage.

Full Knowledge: We would have to know that what we are doing is seriously wrong and against God's law.

Deliberate Consent: We would have to make a free, deliberate decision to commit the sin.

Making the right moral choices

Here are a few 'real life' situations that are fairly typical of what we can meet almost every day. At Confirmation, the Holy Spirit will help us to bear witness to Jesus Christ and to recognize the choices that are open to us. This does not mean that decisions will suddenly become easier for us from now on, in fact they may well get tougher! This is because we are able to see more clearly where our conscience is leading us but we are still free to ignore it. We need courage to answer the challenge of our Lord's invitation: "Come, follow me."

What SHOULD you do?
What WOULD you do?

1 After you leave the music megastore with your new C.D's, you realise that the girl on the checkout has undercharged you by £20. Your friends say "Well done!" Do you:

a) go back to the shop, tell her what happened and pay up?

b) say it was her own stupid fault and pocket the cash?

2 A couple of friends at school have got in with the wrong crowd. You know they are into drugs. You have tried to warn them off but they just tell you to get lost.
Do you:

a) do nothing and just let them ruin their lives?

b) mention it to a member of staff?

3 You work hard at school and do well; but your class mates start calling you a swot, a bore and a teacher's pet. So you ease off the work and start getting bad reports. Your parents and teachers are worried and tell you that you are wasting your time and talents and messing up your career prospects. You feel guilty but you are back in the gang again, always in and out of trouble over silly things; but it's good fun. Do you:

a) Follow your conscience, get back to work and lose your "friends"?

b) Keep in with the gang, waste your time and ruin your future?

4 You like to serve on the altar; you enjoy going to Mass and Father relies on you. All your friends have stopped coming to Mass; they know where you are on a Sunday morning. They start giving you a hard time at school. Do you:

a) Smile and say you will make up your own mind and not change just to suit them?

b) Give in to their pressure, stop going to Mass and play soccer instead?

"Let your light shine before others, ... so that they may give glory to your Father in heaven." (Matthew 5.16) **43**

repentance
(CCCC 1443-1445, 1468 -9)

and reconciliation

Repentance means being sorry for our sins

Repentance means that we really want to change our life, turn away from our sins and follow Jesus. We ask forgiveness from God in the Sacrament of Penance (Confession). At Mass, we say the Our Father and ask our Heavenly Father to forgive our sins as we forgive those who have sinned against us; this can be difficult. We then exchange a sign of peace with each other to show that we mean what we say.

John the Baptist preaches a baptism of repentance

John called people to repent of their sins to prepare for the coming of the Messiah.

"John the baptizer appeared in the wilderness, proclaiming a baptism of repentance for the forgiveness of sins." (Mark 1.4)

(John said) "I baptize you with water for repentance, but one who is more powerful than I is coming after me ... He will baptize you with the Holy Spirit and fire." (Matthew 3.11)

Jesus preaches a baptism of repentance

"Jesus came out of Galilee, proclaiming the good news and saying, 'The time is fulfilled and the kingdom of God has come near, repent and believe the good news.'" (Mark 1.15)

Jesus washed people in the river Jordan as a sign that they wanted to be cleansed of their sins. (John 3.22) This ritual ceremony was already familiar to the Jews, although it was not the Sacrament of Baptism. When Jesus received Baptism from John, his Heavenly Father confirmed him in his life's mission:

"... when Jesus also had been baptized and was praying, the heaven was opened and the Holy Spirit descended upon him in bodily form like a dove. And a voice came from heaven: 'You are my Son, the Beloved; with you I am well pleased.'" (Luke 3.21 - 22)

Jesus gives the apostles power and authority to forgive sins in his name

Jesus goes out of his way to eat with sinners as a gesture of reconciliation; and after he had risen from the dead he appeared to his apostles and gave them power to forgive sins:

"Jesus came and stood among them and said, 'Peace be with you.' ... He breathed on them and said to them, 'Receive the Holy Spirit. If you forgive the sins of any, they are forgiven them: if you retain the sins of any, they are retained.'" (John 20.19-23)

Reconciliation means forgiving others and receiving forgiveness from others

Jesus showed us what reconciliation means when he had a meal at the home of a repentant tax-collector called Zacchaeus. The man confessed in public that he had sinned by defrauding people and he promised to make up for his sins by repaying what he had stolen.

"Jesus said to him, 'Today salvation has come to this house, because he too is a son of Abraham. For the Son of Man came to seek out and save the lost.'" (Luke 19.9 - 10)

When we are reconciled we are at peace with God, with our conscience and with each other. Damaged relationships are mended; we are healed of bitterness and hatred; and so the Sacrament of Penance is called the Sacrament of Reconciliation. The parable of the Prodigal Son (Luke 15. 11-32) and the account of Jesus' conversation with the woman taken in adultery (John 8.3-11) are powerful examples of reconciliation.

The Apostles preach repentance and reconciliation

Both Peter and Paul insisted on the importance of reconciliation:

"They said ... 'Brothers, what should we do?' Peter said 'Repent and be baptised every one of you in the name of Jesus Christ so that you may be forgiven.'" (Acts 2.38)

"...in Christ God was reconciling the world to himself, not counting their trespasses against them, and entrusting the message of reconciliation to us. So we are ambassadors for Christ, since God is making his appeal through us; we entreat you on behalf of Christ, be reconciled to God." (2 Corinthians. 5.19 - 20)

"The kingdom of God has come near; repent and believe in the good news." (Mark 1.15)

friendship & forgiveness

(CCC 1434-1437, 2608)

Good friends are not easy to find. A real friend is someone we can trust, someone who understands us and we can relax with and be ourselves. Forgiveness is an important part of friendship. Even after a big row friends will forgive each other. Families are very important because that is where we learn the meaning of love, forgiveness, friendship, patience and tolerance.

Jesus teaches us about friendship

Our Lord had many friends, called disciples. The word means a learner or a pupil. They shared his company, listened to his preaching and witnessed his many miracles. From among this group Jesus then chose twelve whom he called apostles. An apostle is a messenger, representative, someone sent out. Three out of these twelve , Peter, James and John were particularly close to Christ. They were present when some spectacular events occurred. They were with our Lord when he raised the daughter of Jairus from the dead and when he was transfigured on Mount Tabor. Despite these amazing experiences the friends of Jesus were not always loyal to him.

Jesus teaches us about forgiveness

The really difficult thing about forgiveness is that our Lord tells us that we must always be ready to forgive, not just our friends and family but even our enemies and those who hate us. He insisted that we must forgive others if we wish to be forgiven ourselves:

> "Then Peter came and said to him 'Lord, if my brother sins against me,how often should I forgive? As many as seven times?' Jesus said to him 'Not seven times, but, I tell you, seventy-seven times.'"
> (Matthew 18.21 - 22)

When the adulterous woman was brought before Jesus, the crowd wanted her to be stoned to death. Instead of condemning her to death, Jesus tells her accusers that the person who has never ever sinned should cast the first stone at her.. They all walk away, because they know that everyone is a sinner. Jesus did not condemn her; he simply said:

> "Neither do I condemn you. Go ...do not sin again."
> (John 8.11)

Jesus is abandoned by his friends

Most of the apostles abandoned Our Lord and fled when he was arrested. He still forgave them. Only Saint John with Our Lady and a few of the women followers stayed with Jesus until the end. In the Garden of Gethsemane he actually greeted Judas Iscariot as a friend when he came to betray him with the kiss of greeting and friendship. Later, even Peter the chosen leader denied Jesus three times publicly in the High Priest's house:

> "Another man insisted saying,'This fellow was certainly with him. Why, he is a Galilean.' Peter said,' My friend, I do not know what you are talking about.' At that instant, while he was still speaking, the cock crowed, and the Lord turned and looked straight at Peter, and Peter remembered the Lord's words, 'Before the cock crows today, you will have disowned me three times.' And he went out and wept bitterly." (Luke 22.59 - 62)

Jesus forgives as he is dying on the cross

Jesus forgave those who crucified him, and promised paradise to the repentant thief::

> "They crucified Jesus with the criminals, one on his right and one on his left. Then Jesus said, 'Father, forgive them; for they do not know what they are doing.'" (Luke 23.33 - 34)

> "One of the criminals said,' Jesus, remember me when you come into your kingdom.' Jesus replied, 'Truly, I tell you, today you will be with me in paradise.'" (Luke 23.42 - 43)

"If you forgive the sins of any, they are forgiven them." (John 20.23)

penance
Sacrament of Healing and Forgiveness

(CCC1440 -1470)

We prepare for Confession

We begin our preparation for the sacrament by asking Our Lord for help. Some people say a favourite prayer; others just talk to God in their hearts or maybe use a short prayer like this:

*"Lord, help me to make a good confession,
to know my sins and to be sorry for them.
Help me to serve you better from now on. Amen."*

The Ten Commandments
These ten commandments, and the other laws that accompany them are similar to some of the moral codes that existed in neighbouring civilizations at that time (6th century B.C.). However, what makes the ten commandments unique is that they are the direct words of God himself to Moses; they are short, clear commands; they are more detailed and precise; and in particular they insist on the duty to worship *only one true God*.

Next we examine our conscience. We look back over the time since our last confession to see in what ways we may have failed to serve God. If we examine our conscience when we say our night prayers it will help us to remember.

The Ten Commandments

God gave the ten commandments to Moses as a map of life for his chosen people, the Israelites. We can use the commandments to help us examine our conscience.

The Ten Commandments

The Decalogue (Exodus 20.1-17)

1) You shall not have strange gods before me. You shall not make for yourself a graven image, nor the likeness of anything that is in heaven above or in the earth beneath, nor of those things that are in the waters under the earth, you shall not adore them nor serve them.

2) You shall not take the name of the Lord your God in vain.

3) Remember to keep holy the Lord's day.

4) Honour your father and your mother.

5) You shall not kill.

7) You shall not steal.

8) You shall not bear false witness against your neighbour.

9) You shall not covet your neighbour's wife.

10) You shall not covet your neighbour's goods.

The two main commandments of the Law

Our Lord said that he had come to complete and make perfect the Old Testament Law of Moses.

He summed up the ten commandments in two short rules. These will also help us examine our conscience:

• Love God above everyone and everything else.

• Love your neighbour as you love yourself.

An Examination of Conscience

Do I use God's name with respect? Do I trust in God?

Do I give time each day to pray? Do I listen to God?

Do I pray for others, those who are sick or in trouble?

Do I thank God for his goodness? Do I use my talents?

Do I attend Mass reverently and receive Communion with faith and devotion?

Do I love and obey my parents whatever my age?

Do I criticize, judge or mock others behind their back?

Do I try to help others, especially the vulnerable?

Do I respect God's gift of life and look after my health, or do I damage it with solvents, drugs, tobacco, alcohol or bad diet? Am I lazy?

Do I waste time or disrupt others at school or work?

Am I always courteous and kind to others?

Do I discipline my use of TV and IT technology?

Do I respect my sexuality and that of others?

Am I pure and chaste in mind and body?

Do I show off to others by crude talk and behaviour?

Do I steal - from school, shops or work?

Do I respect private and public property or vandalize it by graffiti or deliberate damage?

Do I frighten others by noisy or threatening behaviour?

Am I irritable, bad tempered, jealous, impatient?

Do I forgive and forget or do I harbour grudges?

Do I always tell the truth or do I lie to avoid trouble?

Do I always thank those who help me?

Do I respect God's gift of Life on all pro-Life issues?

Do I support the poor at home and abroad?

Do I act responsibly to protect the environment?

Jesus Christ, Son of the living God, have mercy on me, a sinner.

we celebrate the
sacrament of penance

We confess our sins to the priest and he gives us a penance.

We make our act of contrition and the priest forgives (absolves) our sins in Jesus' name.

We begin our Confession

We go to the priest and sit or kneel beside him. He may say a few words of welcome. Then we make the sign of the cross and say:

> "In the name of the Father † and of the Son and of the Holy Spirit. Amen.
>
> Bless me, Father, for I have sinned. It is (approximate time) since my last confession."

The priest may then say a short prayer for us:

> *May God who has enlightened every heart, help you to know your sins and trust in his mercy.*

Now we mention our sins. At the end we can say:

> "This is all I can remember." **or** "This is what I wanted to say." **or** "For these and all my other sins which I cannot now remember, I am very sorry and ask pardon of God and penance and absolution from you, Father."

Father may offer a few words of encouragement. This is a good time to ask advice about any problems that may be troubling us. He will then give us a penance, usually a short prayer, to show that we are sorry; it is called *making satisfaction for our sins*. We should always complete the penance we have been given when we come out of confession.

We make an act of Contrition

To acknowledge our sinfulness before God is an act of humility. A parent knows when a child is sorry, but for the sake of the child, still expects the child to say sorry. There is much more to this than good manners. Jesus wants us all to be reconciled with each other and with Almighty God. That is why we make an act of contrition before our sins are forgiven.

> "O my God, because you are so good, I am sorry for all my sins and with the help of your grace, I will not sin again." *or* "O God, be merciful to me, a sinner."

The priest says the words of absolution

The priest raises his right hand and forgives our sins with these words of absolution:

> *God the Father of mercies, through the death and resurrection of his Son, has reconciled the world to himself and sent the Holy Spirit among us for the forgiveness of sins. Through the ministry of the Church, may God give you pardon and peace, and I absolve you from your sins in the name of the Father † and of the Son and of the Holy Spirit. Amen.*

The priest may close the celebration with these few words:

Priest: *Give thanks to the Lord for he is good.*

We reply: "His mercy/love endures for ever."

Priest: *The Lord has freed you from your sins. Go in peace.*

We reply: "Thanks be to God."

your questions about confession

Q) Why do I have to tell my sins to a priest?

A) We tell our sins to a priest in confession because Our Lord told his apostles to forgive sins in his name:

"The disciples were filled with joy at seeing the Lord, and he ... breathed on them and said: 'Receive the Holy Spirit. If you forgive anyone's sins, they are forgiven; if you retain anyone's sins they are retained.'"

(John 20.222 - 23)

Q) God already knows my sins before I tell them, so why should I bother with confession?

A) True, God certainly knows us far better than we shall ever know ourselves. In confession we receive God's forgiveness and we receive his grace to start again. We all have feet of clay. We need to confess our sins and to know that we are forgiven. We need to admit that we have done wrong. We need to take personal responsibility for breaking God's law.

Saint Paul describes the Christian community as the Body of Christ; Jesus is the head and we are the various members of his spiritual body. If one of the members of the body becomes ill through sin, then the whole body suffers. So, in addition to damaging our relationship with God, sin also damages our relationship with each other. That is why Confession reconciles us to the Church and also to God. When we receive Holy Communion we share in the life of the risen Christ and we are united with him and with each other in a special way.

Q) If I had not been to confession for years and had lived an evil life, would I get a hard time from the priest?

A) Not at all. You would receive the same welcome as everyone else. The priest is there in the person of Christ to help us be sorry for our sins and to give us the healing love and forgiveness of our Lord.

Q) Do priests go to confession?

A) Yes. Priests, religious men and women, nuns, monks, bishops and even the pope himself - all are weak human beings and all need to receive forgiveness for their sins in the sacrament of penance/confession.

Q) Will the priest be shocked at what I might have to confess?

A) No chance. The priest is a sinner himself. He is well aware of the weakness of human nature and will have probably heard far more serious sins than those we confess.

Q) Can the priest tell anyone what I have said?

A) Definitely not. The priest is strictly forbidden to disclose anything we mention during confession. This obligation to total secrecy is very serious indeed. It may never be broken. It is called the *Seal of Confession*.

Q) How often should we go to confession?

A) We must go to confession when our conscience tells us that we have seriously offended Almighty God by mortal sin. Some people like to go to confession quite frequently and just mention their main faults and failings. They receive the grace of the sacrament and are drawn closer to our Lord. This would be called a *devotional confession*. Nowadays, people go to confession less often than in the past.

Q) Why do some people say that you should go to confession every time you go to Holy Communion?

A) This pious custom used to be routine for earlier generations, but it is not necessary. It may well have been a result of over - zealous teaching of religious knowledge. We are obliged to go to confession only if we have serious sin on our conscience.

Q) I seem to mention the same old sins every time I go to confession. How can I possibly be sincere if I keep repeating them?

A) Most us probably do not commit grave or mortal sins very often in our lives. But we all have different weaknesses of character. We can be greedy, selfish, jealous, unkind, angry or impatient every day. When we humbly confess these sins we realise our need for the help and forgiveness of Almighty God.

Q) What if I need confession but I am too embarrassed because the priest knows me?

A) You can tell the priest your situation and he will reassure you about the secrecy of the sacrament. However, if there were a situation where the seal of confession might possibly be compromised, you can make an act of sorrow and wait until you have the opportunity to visit another church and speak to a priest who does not know you.

Q) How can my sorrow be genuine if I know that I am almost certain to commit the same sins again and again?

A) Jesus said we must forgive each other seventy times seven times. He is also ready to forgive us however often we may fail to serve him. When we make our act of contrition in confession, we are asking pardon for past sins, not for future possible or likely ones.

Q) Confession seems to have different names. Why is that?

A) This sacrament has become known by three different names:

1) CONFESSION: This word is used because we confess or tell our sins to the priest; and we confess and thank God for his loving mercy.

2) RECONCILIATION: This word is used because, when we go to confession, we are reconciled with the Church, with Almighty God and with each other.

3) PENANCE: This word emphasises our sorrow for sins, our desire to change our lives and to make up in some way for breaking God's law. When we accept the penance, this shows our sincere desire to repent and start again.
(Catechism of the Catholic Church 1423)

"Confession is an act of honesty and courage." (Pope John Paul II)

the sacrament of penance

- an outline history

The Early Church

It took almost fifteen hundred years for the Sacrament of Penance to reach the form with which we are familiar today. In the Gospels and Acts of Apostles we simply read of sins being forgiven. For the first three hundred years, those who sinned after Baptism could receive forgiveness in the Sacrament of Penance only once in their lifetime. Some even said that there were three serious sins that could not be forgiven at all; these were apostasy (this means denying one's Faith) murder, and adultery. Those who committed these sins had to remain penitents for the rest of their lives.

Strict Discipline

It could take a long period of preparation before converts to Christianity were baptised. Many delayed baptism until they were near death, lest they sin again and be barred from receiving Holy Communion. Those who needed forgiveness (called *absolution*) after baptism confessed their sins to the bishop and accept from him a period of public penance which could last for several years. When completed, the bishop would reconcile the sinners to the community and forgive their sins.

Penances were severe and included prayer, fasting, almsgiving and service to the sick. Penitents had to leave Mass before the beginning of the Eucharistic Prayer. One problem arising from this strict approach to the sacrament was the abuse whereby severe penances could be replaced by a hefty fine or a donation to the Church. This meant that wealthy sinners could receive pardon for their sins more easily than the poor; so forgiveness came at a price. As time passed, there was a gradual softening in this severe practice but no one was refused absolution and Holy Communion on their deathbed.

Influence of the Celtic Church

Significant changes began to take place in the 6th century under the influence of the Irish and Welsh monasteries. The Celtic monastic custom was for the monks to confess their sins privately to their abbot, sometimes quite frequently. The abbot would give spiritual guidance as well as a suitable penance before absolving them from their sins. Although this change from public to private confession was a welcome shift, the penances given to the monks were still quite severe by present day standards.

This approach gained general favour with the laity as the humiliation of doing public penance was replaced by private confession to a priest or bishop. The sacrament gradually became available on request and was no longer restricted to just once in a lifetime. A set form was agreed for the prayer of absolution and this practice was eventually adopted throughout the universal Church.

Later Developments

Despite these welcome improvements, the whole process of seeking absolution remained a difficult experience compared with present day custom. The clergy were given prepared lists of sins together with their severity and the appropriate penance to be given. The priest was seen very much as a judge rather than as a healer of souls.

Over the next five hundred years there was a general shift of emphasis away from the judgmental process to an inner conversion of the penitent's mind and heart. The Gospel call to repentance means being sorry for our sins and resolving to make a fresh start. This was how Jesus approached sinners; he was full of compassion and forgiveness for them, while at the same time, challenging them to a radical change of their behaviour and telling them to sin no more.

More recent changes

From the 16th century until 1974, the sacrament of penance changed comparatively little in the way it was administered. Many people still found that going to confession was too impersonal and intimidating. Then in 1974 the Rite of Penance was revised to show more clearly that the sacrament is about receiving the healing and forgiveness of our Lord.

Among the changes introduced perhaps the most welcome is the use of the vernacular instead of Latin; penitents can now hear the words of absolution in their own language. The room itself (the confessional) is better lit and the atmosphere generally more welcoming. There is often an element of choice of place - visible but still secret - either in the body of the church or in the private confessional room; there is the option of sitting or kneeling for confession and the ability to speak face to face with the priest if so desired. All these changes have been generally welcomed by most Catholics, but they have not halted the general decline in the number of people who come to confession. The former practice of regular and frequent confession has declined throughout the U.K. Pope John Paul II lamented this fact as a reflection of the general lack of a sense of sin in the secular atmosphere of contemporary western culture.

The Future

There has been some discussion about the possibility of replacing individual confession with a form of general absolution within a penitential service. However, it seems that the Church is unlikely to change its present practice of allowing general absolution only in the most extreme circumstances, e.g. in time of war. When penitential services are held, often during Advent or Lent, several priests are usually available so that individual sacramental confession may be offered to those who seek the consolation and guidance of sacramental absolution.

"Reconciliation is a fundamental part of the Church's life and mission." (Pope John Paul II)

we make our act of faith

The Creed is a profession of faith.

We say what we believe about God. First, we need to look at some different ideas about faith.

Why do we need the Creed?

Since the early Church, Christians have found it helpful to have a short summary of their religion. (This was called a *Creed* - from the Latin *Credo* which means *I believe*.) The Creed was easy to remember and useful if people enquired about their beliefs. It gradually became longer and more detailed as further clarification of the Gospel message was needed. Both the Apostles' creed and the Nicene creed, share the same plan. Each is divided into three sections, one for each person of the Blessed Trinity.

Can we prove that God exists?

There have been many attempts to prove that God must exist. None of them can be called proofs in the scientific sense. Apart from any other reason, the notion of an infinite being just cannot be understood or contained in our limited human minds. We need the gift of faith. Despite this substantial drawback, various 'proofs' or pointers have emerged over the centuries that some have found helpful. Among the best known of these are the five "ways" offered by Saint Thomas Aquinas, the great 13th century Dominican theologian.

One of his arguments is based on the idea of causality. Everything that exists has a cause; God is the only uncaused cause. Another "way" is the evidence of planned, intelligent design in creation. The mysterious universe in which we live - with its breathtaking beauty, order, colour, together with the scientific laws which govern matter - all point to an intelligent and loving creator.

What is faith? What do we mean when we say "I believe"?

Faith is when we accept something as true because we trust the person who told us. The more reliable the person is, the more confident we can be that what he or she says is true. When people talk about faith, they usually mean religious faith - belief in God or in some intelligent creative power. Non-believers (atheists, some agnostics and most humanists) cannot understand how people can accept religious truths "on faith".

Natural Faith - it is reasonable to believe other people

Faith and trust are really part of our everyday lives. We are making acts of what we can call *natural faith* all the time. It is a normal part of everyday life. If we did not believe or trust people then the whole social fabric of everyday life, relationships at home and work, would collapse.

For example, we rely on, we 'believe' and accept the accuracy of train and plane time-tables, the instructions on the goods we buy

and the information in the yellow pages. We accept as true, we 'believe' the laws of nature and physics; we ignore them at our peril. These few examples of *natural* faith show that it is reasonable to believe and trust information supplied by other people.

The snag here is that not *all* the information we receive is true or reliable. Exaggerated advertising, sensational news headlines and politicians' promises at election time have to be treated with healthy scepticism. We cannot always believe them. So, this *natural* faith can be misplaced; we need to check it out. But, for example, when our doctor tells us the results of our medical tests, we can have confidence that what he or she tells us is true. This is because we *trust* our doctor; we *have faith in*, we *believe* our doctor.

Supernatural Faith - given to us at Baptism

The first thing to remember is that *supernatural* faith is a gift from God. We cannot earn it, but we can be in a position to receive it if we honestly seek the truth with a clear conscience. This is what sometimes happens when an adult from a non-faith or from another religious background wishes to become a member of the Catholic community.

Catholics, and Christians generally, believe that we receive this gift of *supernatural* faith when we are baptized. There is an even stronger reason for us to believe when we know it is God who is speaking to us. This enables us to believe in God and in the teachings of his Divine Son, Jesus Christ. This is because God cannot lie. So when we genuflect before the Blessed Sacrament in the tabernacle, we are making an act of *supernatural* or *religious* faith in the Real Presence of Jesus Christ the Son of God.

The expression *Supernatural Faith* has two meanings: the first is the supernatural gift we receive at Baptism, and the second is everything that God has told us in the Gospels and what he tells us through the teaching guidance of his Church.

the apostles' creed

The first part speaks of God the Father, the first person of the Blessed Trinity.

The second part speaks of Jesus Christ, the second person of the Blessed Trinity. The third part speaks of the Holy Spirit, the third person of the Blessed Trinity. Let us now take a closer look at each section of the Apostles' Creed.

The Apostles' Creed

This concise summary of our Christian Faith dates back to the time of the apostles. An early claim that it had actually been written by them, with each apostle contributing one of the twelve sections, was dismissed as a pious legend by medieval scholars. However, we do know that the text reflects the teaching and 'mind' of the apostles. By the early 3rd century it was being used by catechumens, who recited it before receiving Baptism. St. Ambrose, bishop of Milan, mentions a Creed in A.D. 390 which had been in use for nearly two hundred years and was based on a Creed used in Rome.

The Nicene Creed

This is the profession of Faith we recite at Sunday Mass. It dates from the Council of Nicea in modern Turkey, in A.D. 325. The bishops wanted to make it clear that Jesus Christ is truly God as well as truly man. The theologian Arius and others were denying this at the time. The council of Constantinople (Istanbul) in A.D. 381, revised the text and clarified that the Holy Spirit is also truly God, together with the Father and the Son. This emphasizes our belief in the Blessed Trinity. The Creed contains truths of our Faith that are too difficult for us fully to understand. They are called mysteries.

The Apostles' Creed

Part one:
    I believe in God,
    the Father Almighty,
    Creator of heaven and earth.

Part two:
    And in Jesus Christ,
    his only Son, our Lord,
    who was conceived by the Holy Spirit,
    born of the Virgin Mary,
    suffered under Pontius Pilate,
    was crucified, died and was buried.
    He descended into hell;
    the third day he rose again from
    the dead.
    He ascended into heaven;
    and is seated at the right hand of God
    the Father Almighty;
    He will come again
    to judge the living and the dead.

Part three
    I believe in the Holy Spirit;
    the holy Catholic Church;
    the communion of saints;
    the forgiveness of sins;
    the resurrection of the body;
    and life everlasting. Amen.

The Nicene Creed

Part one:
    We believe in one God,
    the Father, the Almighty, maker of heaven and earth,
    of all that is, seen and unseen.

Part two:
    We believe in one Lord, Jesus Christ,
    the only Son of God, eternally begotten of the Father,
    God from God, Light from Light,
    true God from true God, begotten not made,
    of one being with the Father.
    Through him all things were made.
    For us men and for our salvation he came down from heaven:
    by the power of the Holy Spirit he became incarnate
    of the Virgin Mary, and was made man.
    For our sake he was crucified under Pontius Pilate;
    he suffered death and was buried.
    On the third day he rose again in accordance with the
    Scriptures;
    he ascended into heaven
    and is seated at the right hand of the Father.
    He will come again in glory
    to judge the living and the dead,
    and his kingdom will have no end.

Part three
    We believe in the Holy Spirit, the Lord, the giver of life,
    who proceeds from the Father and the Son.
    With the Father and the Son he is worshipped and glorified.
    He has spoken through the prophets.
    We believe in one holy catholic and apostolic Church.
    We acknowledge one baptism for the forgiveness of sins.
    We look for the resurrection of the dead,
    and the life of the world to come. Amen.

"The Creed ... is a summary of the principal truths of the faith." (CCC188)

I believe in God, the father almighty

(CCC 185 -278)

There is one God

Three great world religions, Christianity, Judaism and Islam, all believe that there is only one God. We believe that God is infinite. There is no limit to God's loving power, justice, beauty and truth. God is eternal; he has no beginning or end. God is the supreme mystery who will always be beyond our human understanding.

God reveals his name to Moses on Mount Horeb

When God told Moses that he was sending him to Pharaoh to lead his people out of slavery in Egypt, Moses was understandably anxious:

> "Moses said to God, 'If I come to the Israelites and say to them
> 'The God of our ancestors has sent me to you,' and they ask me,
> 'What is his name?' what shall I tell them?' God said to Moses,
> 'I AM WHO I AM'. He said further,
> 'Thus you shall say to the Israelites,
> ' I AM has sent me to you.'"
> (Exodus 3.13-14)

God tells his chosen people about himself

This passage is held in great reverence by devout Jews:

> "Hear O Israel: The Lord is our God, the Lord alone. You shall love the Lord your God with all your heart and with all your soul and with all your might. Keep these words that I am commanding you today in your heart. Recite them to your children and talk about them, when you lie down and when you rise. Bind them as a sign on your hand, fix them as an emblem on your forehead, and write them on the doorposts of your house and on your gates."
> (Deuteronomy 6.4-9)

When Jesus is asked which is the most important commandment of the Law, he quotes the same passage but adds the further commandment - to love our neighbour as ourselves. (Mark 12.29 - 32)

Jesus uses the divine name about himself

Jesus spoke about Almighty God as his Father; clearly claiming that in some way he is like God. On more than one occasion, when he was talking with the Pharisees, Jesus uses the divine name about himself. When he spoke about his approaching death, he used the Old Testament name that God had revealed to Moses. The Jewish leaders wanted to stone him to death for blasphemy:

> "Jesus said, 'When you have lifted up the Son of Man, then you will realise that I AM HE.'" .... "Jesus said to them, 'Very truly, I tell you, before Abraham was, I AM,"
> (John 8.28, 58)

"Jesus said ...'for God all things are possible.'" (Matthew 19.26)

creator of heaven and earth (CCC 279 -421)

God is the creator of everything

We believe that almighty God made the whole universe and everything in it from nothing. During the Easter Vigil celebration, the first reading of the Liturgy of the Word recalls the Genesis account of the creation:

"In the beginning when God created the heavens and the earth, darkness covered the face of the deep, while the spirit of God swept over the face of the waters." (Genesis 1.1-2)

God's creation shows his power and love

The universe is good because it is created by the goodness of God:

"God saw everything that he had made, and indeed, it was very good." (Genesis 1.31)

Angels - an unseen part of God's creation (CCC 185 -278)

We believe that God has created purely spiritual beings which the bible calls angels. They are mentioned in the Nicene Creed as "all things, seen and unseen." The word angel means a servant or messenger. These pure spirits are intelligent immortal beings. They are mentioned in the Gospels:

- The angel Gabriel announced the birth of Our Lord. (Luke 1.26)
- They sang at the birth of Christ. (Luke 2.13 - 14)
- An angel consoled Our Lord in Gethsemane. (Luke 22.43)
- An angel announced the resurrection. (Matthew 28.5)
- Jesus speaks of them. (Matthew 18.10, 26.53.)
- Catholic tradition holds that the guardian angels help us in our lives.

The human race

We are the highest form of life in the universe; a unique fusion of matter and spirit, part physical, part spiritual. We can think, feel, communicate and love in a way which makes us distinct from the rest of creation. We are God's favourite creatures, made in his image. We are the only creatures who can know and love God. At the same time we are also made from the dust of the earth and will return to dust when we die. Yet our spiritual soul is immortal. It cannot die; and

we are destined to live for ever in the presence of God. This is our faith.

Why does God allow suffering? - The Problem of Evil

If God is infinitely loving and powerful, why do millions of innocent children die of poverty and disease? Why does he allow cruelty, wars or natural disasters? Why do the wicked go unpunished while good people suffer?

The problem has challenged mankind for thousands of years. It crops up in different forms in early writings, including the Bible - in the psalms and the books of Wisdom and Job. Life is full of uncertainties and contradictions. We all experience grief and suffering. There are no easy answers. When we see terrible evil, we all have to admit that "There, but for the grace of God, go I."

Against all this evil, we have the shining example of millions of people who live lives of selfless goodness. They have chosen freely to follow their conscience and to serve God and their neighbour. God asks each of us to accept our cross in humility and faith, and to trust that he will turn all our suffering into good in the fullness of time. Jesus said:

"If any want to become my followers, let them deny themselves and take up their cross and follow me." (Matthew 16.24)

How did the universe begin?

Most of us, and especially scientists, irrespective of our religious beliefs, are fascinated by the search for the origins of the universe and of life. Catholics believe that God is the Creator who is the ultimate Uncaused Cause of matter, energy and life itself, while acknowledging the role of evolution in God's creative plan. Even if the seemingly endless series of scientific challenges were to be explained about the origins of the universe, another equally challenging question remains: Why does the universe exist at all?
Catholics believe that faith can answer this question.

Faith and Reason

We believe that all truth, goodness and beauty is found in God. When we study any area of knowledge - the great intellectual disciplines of religion, philosophy, the sciences, art and literature - there should be no conflict or contradiction between scientific truth and religious faith and morality, because all have their origin in God.
Sadly, history shows that this is far from being accepted by all scholars. Many scientists reject religious faith and the idea of an objective moral law - i.e. an unchanging law of right and wrong. They dismiss the idea as completely irrelevant because religious opinions and moral laws may limit intellectual freedom by seeking to restrict the boundaries of scientific research. Many scientists demand freedom to experiment with human embryos with cloning and stem cell research, and seek to justify abortion and euthanasia, without being restrained by any ethical or moral restraints or standards. Despite this, there are many of the world's top scientists who are men and women of profound religious faith and who reject this atheistic approach to the sanctity of human life, and the mentality that would exclude religious faith from the search for knowledge. We should remember that Faith and Knowledge are two different but complementary ways of approaching and understanding truth. Intellectual knowledge needs religious faith to maintain respect for human dignity. Religious faith needs rigorous intellectual discipline to maintain respect for critical research.

the blessed trinity
three persons in one God
(CCC 232 - 264)

The Sign of the Cross

Since the 2nd Century, Christians have made the sign of the cross as an act of faith in the Three Divine Persons in the Blessed Trinity. When we bless ourselves with holy water and say: "In the name of the Father and of the Son and of the Holy Spirit" we are making the same act of faith in the most profound mystery at the heart of the Godhead and at the heart of our Catholic life. Christians believe that there are three divine persons in the one God, Father, Son and Holy Spirit. This is not part of the Jewish or Muslim faith.

The Gospels speak of three Divine Persons

The Gospels often refer to the Father and the Holy Spirit:

"... Jesus answered them,' My Father is still working and I also am working.' For this reason the Jews were seeking all the more to kill him because he was not only breaking the Sabbath, but he was also calling God his own Father, thereby making himself equal to God."
(John 5.17 - 18)

"The Father and I are one." "The Father is in me and I am in the Father." "Whoever has seen me has seen the Father."
(John 10.30,38; 14.9)

"Suddenly the heavens were opened to him and he saw the Spirit of God descending like a dove and alighting on him. And a voice from heaven said, 'This is my beloved Son with whom I am well pleased.'"
(Matthew 3.16 - 17)

After his baptism, Jesus went into the wilderness to pray and prepare for his life's work of preaching the Good News and doing the will of his heavenly Father. These quotations show that Jesus is united with his Heavenly Father and the Holy Spirit:

"Jesus, full of the Holy Spirit, returned to the Jordan and was led by the Spirit into the wilderness." (Luke 4.1)

Jesus proclaims the Blessed Trinity

The last words of the risen Jesus to his Apostles on the Mount of Olives before he ascended to heaven, speak clearly of three Divine Persons:

"Go therefore and make disciples of all nations, baptizing them in the name of the Father and of the Son and of the Holy Spirit, and teaching them to obey everything that I have commanded you."
(Matthew 28.19)

"The mystery of the Most Holy Trinity is the central mystery of the Christian faith." (CCC261)

... and in Jesus Christ, his only son, our lord, who was conceived by the holy spirit, born of the Virgin Mary

(CCC 422 -570)

The Mystery of the Incarnation

The Second Person of the Blessed Trinity took human nature in Jesus Christ. This is called the Incarnation. He was born of the Virgin Mary through the power of the Holy Spirit. Jesus is both truly God and truly man.

> "The Word became flesh and lived among us." (John 1.14)

The birth of Jesus at Bethlehem is the most dramatic intervention of God in human history. Jesus Christ, the Son of God, lived on this earth and earned his daily bread as a carpenter. The last three years of his short life were spent in proclaiming the Good News of salvation to all who would listen. He called us to repent of our sins, and get our lives back on the right track. This life prepares us for everlasting life in heaven. Jesus also showed us:

- The dignity of work - we are called to use God's creation responsibly.
- The duty to use our gifts from God - we all have our own path to God.
- God is with us all the way - we are never alone when serving God.

The Annunciation

Mary was completely open to God's will when she was asked by the angel Gabriel to become the mother of the Messiah. So it was that Jesus Christ was formed within her by the Holy Spirit, and she gave our Redeemer to the world.

We first receive the Holy Spirit when we are baptized. When we are confirmed the Holy Spirit gives us strength to bear witness to Jesus. If we are open to the Holy Spirit we too will be able to bring Our Lord to others by the example of our daily lives; just by the way we live and behave. Saint Paul wrote:

> "It is no longer I who live, but it is Christ who lives in me."
> (Galatians 2.20)

Why did God become man in Jesus Christ?

- to reconcile the world again to our loving Creator. He sacrificed his life to atone for our sins and reconcile us to God:

> "He (John the Baptist) saw Jesus coming toward him and declared, 'Here is the Lamb of God who takes away the sin of the world.'" (John 1.29)

> "God sent his only Son into the world so that we might live through him. In this is love, not that we loved God but that He loved us and sent his Son to be the atoning sacrifice for our sins." (1 John 4.9 - 10)

- to show us by the example of his life how we should love one another:

> "Jesus said to them, ' I am the way and the truth and the life. No one can come to the Father except through me.'

> "This is my commandment ... love one another as I have loved you,"

> "No one has greater love than this, to lay down one's life for one's friends." (John 14.6; 15.12 - 13)

- Saint Paul quotes an early Christian hymn:

> "Though Jesus Christ was in the form of God, he did not count equality with God a thing to be grasped, but emptied himself, taking the form of a servant, being born in the likeness of men. And being found in human form he humbled himself and became obedient unto death, even death on a cross." (Philippians 2..6 -8)

The Church teaches
The Incarnation is therefore the mystery of the wonderful union of the divine and human natures in the one person of the Word. *(Catechism of the Catholic Church 483)*

Mary, Mother of God
We address Our Blessed Lady as "Mother of God" because she is the mother of the eternal Son of God made man, who is God himself. *(Catechism of the Catholic Church 509)*

"And the Word became flesh and lived among us, and we have seen his glory." (John 1.14)

55

Pontius Pilate, was crucified, died and was buried. (CCC 571 - 630)

Pontius Pilate

Pilate was a career soldier in the Roman army. In A.D. 26 he was appointed governor of Judaea, part of the Roman province of Syria. He was an arrogant and brutal man, intolerant of subordinates. In A.D. 36 he was recalled to Rome, to answer before the Emperor for his ruthless and provocative behaviour towards the Jews.

Pilate probably never understoood or cared about the religious issues which so concerned the Jews. For him, religion was merely the science of ritual - completing the required civil ceremonial duties with the burning of incense before a variety of deities. Religion had nothing to do with morality or personal behaviour.

He did however have a basic respect for the rule of law, probably the greatest legacy of the Roman empire. At the same time he was without scruple when it came to political expediency, even when this resulted in a callous disregard for human life. The result was a reign of arbitrary terror.

The devil is the father of lies; and Pilate asks Jesus "What is truth?" Jesus taught that justice always matters - especially to the little people. Pilate knew this very well but chose to ignore it. He compromised on truth, on justice, on the eternal value of human life; and so he condemned to death Jesus, the very author of life itself.

Crucifixion

Crucifixion was a brutal and humiliating form of execution. The victim was first scourged and then forced to carry the cross beam to the place of execution. This beam was then slotted on to the prepared upright stake. The victim was tied and sometimes also nailed to the cross through hands and feet; and had to raise himself by his pierced limbs in order to breathe. It could take several days before the victim died from exhaustion or asphyxiation, unless the legs were broken to hasten the end.

The Problem

The Gospel accounts of the final days of Jesus read like a tragic drama which leads to a stunning and totally unexpected climax. Jesus was loved by the ordinary people. Here was a popular preacher, a healer of all who came to him, broken in body or spirit. His profound wisdom at once baffled and infuriated both the Pharisees and Sadducees. Here was a man who spoke of God as his Father and who rewarded faith by forgiving sin. Such outrageous claims and challenging displays of supernatural power were bound to make enemies among the religious and political leaders of the time.

The Pharisees

One group in particular, the Pharisees, (the 'separated ones') were strict upholders of the purity of the Jewish Law, and felt threatened by the teaching of Jesus. They objected strongly to the way in which he spoke about the Law. One minute he was insisting on respect for every last syllable, and the next he was prepared to cure people and work other miracles on the sabbath, in clear violation of the Law's prohibition of all forms of work on holy days. He even said that "The Son of Man is master even of the sabbath."

They also felt under attack from him for what he called their hypocrisy in applying the law. He said that the extra obligations they had added to the prescriptions of the Law in order to ensure its perfect observance - 'the tradition of the Elders' - had resulted in many people being unable to keep the Law at all. This condemned them to the status of unclean outcasts.

The Sadducees

Another group who felt threatened by the popular preaching of Jesus was the rich and powerful Sadducee party. This aristocratic body of high - priestly families administered the temple worship and finances very much to their own advantage, with the consent of the Roman authorities.

People would comment that, unlike the other rabbis, Jesus taught with authority. This young rabbi, from Nazareth of all places, with no specialist education to speak of, had an awesome knowledge of the Law and undeniable supernatural powers. He was a firebrand with little regard for their authority; and was without fear or respect when he publicly condemned their corrupt management of the temple.

The Solution

Clearly, something had to be done about Jesus the Nazarene, the itinerant preacher, carpenter son of Joseph in Galilee. His growing popularity, his status as a teacher was fast becoming not just an irritating embarrassment but a real threat to the authority of these two powerful groups. A popular uprising in his support, especially at the politically sensitive time of Passover, would bring down the full might of Rome. This would be the end not just of the Nazarene, but also of the high - priestly families and their supporters. There was nothing else for it; the Nazarene would just have to go ...

"This man ... you crucified and killed by the hands of those outside the law." (Acts 2.23)

he descended into hell; the third day he rose from the dead. (CCC 631 - 658)

He descended into hell

Hell is the name given here to the place for all those who have died.*   (Matthew 25.41) When the Creed speaks about Jesus "descended into hell" it just means that he died like any other person. But, as Jesus told Martha:

> "I am the resurrection and the life. Those who believe in me, even though they die, will live."
> (John 11.25)

When we now speak of Hell we usually mean the state of someone who completely rejects God and freely chooses to reject his love and forgiveness. The Church has never said that any single person is in hell. There is always the hope of repentance.

The Resurrection

Jesus rose from the dead as he had promised - the crowning climax of his life; a historical fact, witnessed by hundreds of people and recorded several times in the Gospels. The apostles talked to the risen Christ; they touched his wounds and even ate with him. They knew that he had definitely risen from the dead, although initially they were not easily convinced and they also knew that his physical appearance had changed. Unlike the body of the risen Lazarus, the body of the risen Jesus could not and cannot die again. That is why we say that his risen body was somehow transformed, glorified. At the resurrection we rise with a glorified body which is worthy of the vision of God.

The Resurrection is central to our faith

The resurrection of Jesus is absolutely central to our Catholic Faith. It is not pious hope or an uncertain step into the darkness of make-believe. It is a confident certainty of something which we did not personally witness, but which is nevertheless a fact. This fact is as true as any other historical event and infinitely more important. That is why Saint Paul could write:

> "If there is no resurrection of the dead, then Christ himself cannot have been raised; and if Christ has not been raised then our preaching is useless and your believing it is useless."
> (1 Corinthians 15.13 - 14)

People sometimes ask what the resurrection means and why it is so important for Christians. The answer is clear. God the Son, the Second Person of the Blessed Trinity, took human nature in Jesus Christ. He shared our human condition and offered his life to his Heavenly Father in atonement for our sins. When Jesus rose again from the dead, he restored human nature to the glorious state of union with God which it had before mankind's fall from grace.

The risen Jesus appears to Saul

Saul was a strict Pharisee who persecuted the early Christians. One day, the risen Jesus appeared to him on the road to Damascus. He received Baptism, and, as Paul, he became a fearless missionary. He claimed equal status to the other apostles - because he had seen and spoken with the risen Christ and proclaimed that Jesus had risen from the dead:

> "For I handed on to you as of first importance ...that Christ died for our sins in accordance with the scriptures, and that he was buried, and that he was raised on the third day ... and that he appeared to Cephas, then to the twelve ... Last of all, as to one untimely born, he appeared also to me."
> (1 Corinthians 15.3 - 8)

(*The word 'hell' is the usual English translation of the Aramaic word Gehenna, the place of punishment of the wicked; but the Apostles' Creed uses this word 'Hell' for the general resting place of the dead. The usual word for the resting place for all those who have died is Hades (Hebrew Sheol), but the evangelists themselves are not always consistent in its use.)

Hell
Early ideas about the universe divided the world into three floors - the earth was on the ground floor, heaven was on the top floor, and the underworld or 'kingdom of the dead' was in the cellar. For the Jews Sheol was a joyless place. Later, they came to understand that the good would be rewarded and the wicked punished. One branch of Judaism accepts the doctrine of the resurrection.

The Resurrection
The main element in the early preaching of the apostles was that Jesus is risen from the dead. After the Holy Spirit had come upon them at Pentecost, Peter's message was "Jesus Christ is alive!" and people should repent of their sins and receive Baptism. We would expect the resurrection to be seen by the early church as proof of his divinity, i.e. that Jesus must be God made man. It had happened so recently that it was still vividly impressed on people's memories. They believed that Jesus must be God because he had risen from the dead.
But, as time went by, this approach gradually changed, especially in the second generation of Christians. People began to believe that Jesus had risen from the dead only if they already believed that he is God. In other words, the divinity of Christ was seen as the reason for his rising from the dead and not the other way round. People would say "Jesus rose from the dead because he is God."- they had already made an act of personal faith. They did not say "Jesus must be God because he rose from the dead."

The Resurrection and Faith
This shift in attitude may appear rather strange at first; but we need only recall Jesus' warning in Luke 16.31, "If they will not listen to Moses or to the prophets, they will not be convinced even if someone should rise from the dead." In addition, when Jesus showed his power over death by raising Lazarus from the tomb, this did not persuade the Jewish leaders to believe in him. On the contrary, they began to look for a way to get rid of him for good; and they even planned to get rid of Lazarus as well. This shows that, without the initial faith in the divinity of Our Lord, people refused to accept that he had power over death.

he ascended into heaven; and is seated at the right hand of God the father almighty. (CCC 659 - 667)

Saint Mark tells us that Jesus was "taken up into heaven". (16.19) Matthew just speaks of Jesus commissioning the disciples to preach and baptize, and reminds them that he is with them until the end of time. (28.20) John may suggest (in 17.4 - 5) that the ascension will be the glorification of Jesus by his heavenly Father. Luke's account (24.51) says; "While he was blessing them, he withdrew from them and was carried up to heaven. "

The Paschal Mystery
This is the passion, death, resurrection and ascension of Our Lord. His death frees us from sin; his resurrection means we will rise again and live with him for ever. Jesus was raised up on the cross for our sins. His suffering and death was a triumphant success for us. His ascension, when he was again raised up to his heavenly Father - completes his saving work. Where he has gone, we shall follow. "'And I, when I am lifted up from the earth, will draw all people to myself.' He said this to indicate the kind of death he was to die."

Judgment
Our mortal body decays at death but our immortal soul will live for ever. At death we face the truth about ourselves in the light of Christ; this is sometimes called our "particular judgment". God's justice will be a loving justice. We make our own eternal destiny by the way we have lived. " For with the judgment you make you will be judged, and the measure you give will be the measure you get." (Matthew 7.2)
"Come, you that are blessed by my Father, inherit the kingdom prepared for you ... as you did it to one of the least who are members of my family, you did it to me." (Matthew 25.34,40)

Holy souls in purgatory
It has long been Catholic tradition to pray that those who have died will be cleansed of their sins. This is called intercessory prayer for the holy souls. Purgatory is not a place; it is a time of purification for those who have died, that they may be prepared to enjoy eternal happiness with God in heaven.

Jesus ascends to heaven

In Acts of the Apostles we read that, after his resurrection, Jesus instructed his disciples for forty days. He told them that when they had been empowered by the Holy Spirit, they were to witness to him to the ends of the earth. Then:

"As they watched, he was lifted up, and a cloud took him from their sight." (Acts 1.9)

The Gospels do not say how this happened. Words may simply have failed them; but they do record Jesus' promise to remain with them in his Holy Spirit:

"Stay here in the city until you have been clothed with power from on high." (Luke 24.49)

Seated at the right hand of God the Father

Traditionally, the right hand was the sword hand and therefore the place of honour, power and influence. The prophets spoke of the Messiah being enthroned at the right hand side of God. This is what Saint Peter was talking about when he spoke to the Jerusalem crowds after the Holy Spirit had come upon the apostles at Pentecost:

"This Jesus God raised up, and of that all of us are witnesses. Being therefore exalted at the right hand of God, and having received from the Father the promise of the Holy Spirit, he has poured out this that you both see and hear." (Acts 2.32 - 33)

He will come again to judge the living and the dead. (CCC 668 - 682)

The second coming and the final judgment

We believe that Jesus will come again in glory at the end of time when the final judgment will take place. Saint Paul says that this will not happen until God's chosen Jewish people have accepted that Jesus is the Messiah sent by God. Before this happens the Church will endure a final onslaught of the devil. It took some time for the early Christians to understand that Jesus' second coming is not imminent:

"The Lord is not slow about his promise as some think of slowness, but he is patient with you, not wanting any to perish, but all to come to repentance." (2 Peter 3.9)

In Matthew's Gospel, Jesus uses a popular, prophetic style of preaching which merges recent events with a much broader vision of God's plan. Part of this chapter could refer to the destruction of Jerusalem (A.D.70).

"Then many will fall away and they will betray one another ... And many false prophets will arise and lead many astray ... they will see the Son of Man coming on the clouds of heaven with power and great glory." (Matthew 24.10,30)

"We will all stand before the judgement seat of God." (Romans 13.10)

I believe in the Holy Spirit; the Holy Spirit is at work in all the baptized

(CCC 683 -747)

The Holy Spirit is the third Person of the blessed Trinity. We receive the gift of faith from the Holy Spirit when we are re-born at baptism. The Holy Spirit is active throughout the Church in many ways:

- in the inspired words of holy Scripture and in the teaching of the Church;

- in the Sacraments and the many different priestly and lay ministries;

- in the witness given by good people whose lives are open to the Holy Spirit.

Jesus begins his preaching

The prophet Isaiah speaks of the coming Messiah. Jesus quotes from this prophecy (Isaiah 61.1-2) when he begins to preach the good news:

"The Spirit of the Lord is upon me, because he has anointed me to bring the good news to the poor. He has sent me to proclaim release to the captives and recovery of sight to the blind, to let the oppressed go free, to proclaim the year of the Lord's favour." (Luke 4.18 - 19)

I believe in the holy Catholic Church;

(CCC 748 - 945)

The Church is formed by the Holy Spirit

The Holy Spirit came upon the Apostles at Pentecost. In the Acts of Apostles we read how Peter led the work of preaching the Gospel message. The reaction of the people sums up what the Church is all about and what it still is today.

- They believed the Gospel message.
- They received the sacrament of baptism.
- They met together to pray and break bread.
- They gave alms to those in need.

So the Church is a community of believers, united by the Holy Spirit in baptism and set apart to love and worship God and to serve each other in Christ. (Read about this in Acts 2.37-47)

The four marks of the Church

The Nicene Creed mentions four characteristics of the Church.

The Church is one

The Church proclaims one and the same Gospel message throughout the ages. Its doctrine develops over time as richer truths are discerned after careful discussions. All the bishops and clergy are united in professing the same message under the leadership of the Holy Father, the Pope.

The Church is holy

We give glory to God by the holiness of our lives. The Holy Spirit helps us to grow in holiness when we pray, read the scriptures and receive the sacraments especially Confession and Holy Communion.

The Church is catholic

The original meaning of the word catholic is that the Church is universal; it embraces people of all races and cultures. Since the Reformation the word is used in a narrower sense of the (Roman) Catholic Church as distinct from the Protestant, Baptist and other churches.

The Church is apostolic

The Church began during the time of the apostles and bishops are their successors. The Church's teaching today is faithful to the teaching of the apostles.

I believe in the communion of saints;

(CCC 946 - 962)

The Church is the family of Jesus Christ

The *Communion of Saints* is another description of the Church. Just as the family is our most important social unit, helping us to grow and become happy and mature adults, so also the Church is a family of believers. We are re-born into this family at our Baptism when we share in the supernatural life of Grace, united by the Holy Spirit. Saint Paul says that the Church is the body of Christ in which each of us has a different role to play. Jesus said:

> " I am the vine and you are the branches. Those who abide in me and I in them bear much fruit, because apart from me you can do nothing."
> (John 15.5)

We are drawn closer to Our Lord and to each other when we receive the sacraments, especially the Eucharist.

The Church is a communion of saints, living and dead

Saint Paul calls the Christians at Corinth Saints - because they are a community of the Eucharist and are called to be holy. The Church on earth is united as a community throughout the world. We can see this in Rome and at places of international pilgrimage like Walsingham, Lourdes, or Medjugorge. The saints in heaven are an important part of the Church, especially our Blessed Lady. We pray to the saints that they will intercede for us before God.

Those who have died are also very much part of our family of faith. We pray for them that their sins may be forgiven and that they may soon enjoy the complete happiness of the presence of God.

I believe in the forgiveness of sins; (CCC 976 - 987)

We need to be forgiven

Our journey through life is marked by a great variety of situations. At different times we may experience hopes and fears, happiness and sorrow, pain and suffering, love and longing, injustice, failure or even rejection. Despite living in a wonderful world, we are not always at peace within ourselves. We commit sin when we fail to love God and our neighbour, when we put ourselves and our own interests before other people's and before God's law. Saint Paul says:

> "I do not understand my own actions, for I do not do what I want, but I do the very thing I hate."
> (Romans 7.15)

This is one of the consequences of what is called Original Sin. When we have sinned our conscience reminds us that we have done wrong. We feel guilty, ashamed; we need forgiveness and healing. The Sacrament of Penance reconciles us with the Christian community and with God.

We are reconciled to God through the cross and resurrection of Jesus

We believe that Jesus came to reconcile us to God. This is why the cross is such an important symbol of our Faith. The liturgy of Holy Week is a wonderful celebration of God's love for us and is the most important religious feast in the Church's calendar. Once again Saint Paul reminds us:

> "God proves his love for us in that while we still were sinners Christ died for us .....we even boast in God through our Lord Jesus Christ, through whom we have now received reconciliation."

> "Now that you have been freed from sin and enslaved to God, the advantage you get is sanctification. The end is eternal life."
> (Romans 5.8,11; 6.22)

"The Lord has laid on him the iniquity of us all ." (Isaias 53.6)

I believe in the resurrection of the body: (CCC 988 - 1019)

The last frontier

Popular science magazines often speak about exploration into deep space as the last frontier which challenges the human mind and spirit. But there is another, more fundamental frontier which has challenged us since time began. It is the mystery of life itself. "What does it mean? ... Why do I exist? ... Why must I die? ... What will happen to me when I die?" In 1965 the Second Vatican Council produced a document about the contemporary world. It includes this statement:

"It is in the face of death that the riddle of human existence becomes most acute. Man is tormented ... by a dread of perpetual extinction ... rebels against death because he bears within himself a seed of eternity ...the Church teaches that man has been created by God for a blissful purpose beyond the reach of earthly misery."
(The Church in the World 18)

The Resurrection

"I am the resurrection and the life. Those who believe in me, even though they die, will live, and everyone who lives and believes in me will never die."
(John 11.25 - 26)

From the very beginning, Jesus preached the resurrection of the dead; and his followers also preached it after Pentecost. The human yearning for something beyond this limited world was fulfilled when Jesus rose triumphantly from the grave, to conquer both sin and death. We can now be sure that we shall indeed rise again from the dead in the fullness of time. Thus, one of the most profound mysteries that have challenged the human mind was resolved on the first.

> **The Imitation of Christ**
> Published in 1472 and attributed to Thomas a Kempis, a saintly member of a religious community. It contains short spiritual proverbs, prayers, conversations between the reader and Christ and meditations on the Blessed Sacrament.
>
> **Amen**
> The Hebrew word Amen means "truly...It is true." i.e. we agree with what has been said. Related to the Hebrew for "Believe" it is used of someone who is truthful and trustworthy. Jesus used *Amen* to emphasize that he spoke with God's authority. New translations often substitute its modern equivalent, e.g. "In all truth ... I tell you most solemnly ... *Truly I tell you.*" "So whenever you give alms, do not sound the trumpet before you, as the hypocrites do ...Truly, I tell you, they have received their reward." (Matthew 6.2) In some Free Churches the congregation may feel moved to profess their faith as their pastor proclaims the Gospel with interjections of *Amen!* or *Alleluia!* as the spirit moves. The meaning is the same; viz "Yes! I agree. It is true."

I believe in life everlasting. Amen. (CCC 1020 - 1065)

Eternal Life

Everything that is MORTAL - created - will eventually decay and die. We know that this life will end in our physical death. But God's love gives us ETERNAL life. Just as Jesus rose from the dead, we too will rise to everlasting life. We can make plans and look forward to the future, but we do so in the knowledge that what lies ahead of us is very often beyond our control. As the Imitation of Christ puts it: "Man proposes, God disposes."

Amen

The Amen we say at the end of the Creed repeats and completes the opening words "I believe." It means that we accept God's word as true and we place our complete faith in him. The Amen at the end of our prayers means we believe that God will fulfil his promises. The word Amen is used in both Jewish and Christian worship. At the end of the Eucharistic Prayer, the priest says:

> **"Through him, with him, in him, in the unity of the Holy Spirit all glory and honour is yours, almighty Father, for ever and ever."**

Our response Amen means "Yes! We agree. It is true." Later in the Mass, when we receive Holy Communion, our reply to the priest, deacon or minister when they say "The Body/Blood of Christ" is Amen. It means we believe that Jesus is really and truly present. The last book of the Bible, the Book of Revelation, ends with the same act of faith and trust in God's message:

> "The one who testifies to these things says 'Surely I am coming soon.' Amen. Come Lord Jesus! The grace of the Lord Jesus be with all the saints. Amen."
> (Revelation 22.20 - 21)

prayer ... talking and listening to God

"Prayer is the raising of the mind and heart to God." (St John Damascene)

'Phone a friend

Most people have a mobile phone. It is great to keep in touch with family and friends; a quick call gives instant reassurance and peace of mind. It is easy enough to talk but it is more difficult to listen carefully to what people are telling us. Some of us are great talkers but poor listeners.

Prayer is a bit like that. It gives us instant access to God. He is always on the line, waiting for our call and he never hangs up on us. But we need to listen carefully for his voice in the silence of our heart if we are to hear what he is saying, amid the general hubbub of everyday life. The psalm tells us:

"Harden not your hearts today, but listen to the voice of the Lord." (Psalm 95.7)

God loves me

We all need to be valued and loved. But far deeper than our need for human love is our hunger for God. We shall never be able fully to understand the immensity of God's love for us. When we feel the need to pray, it is the Holy Spirit within us drawing us to our heavenly Father. The whole world is filled with the glory of God. God is all around us and prayer is our link with him. God has given us life, family and friends, gifts and talents. Whenever we turn to God in prayer, we should begin by thanking him for his goodness to us.

Most of us think about Jesus when we pray. Jesus himself told us that no one knows the Father except the Son and those to whom the Son chooses to reveal him. We are reminded of this in the prayers at Mass which are addressed to our heavenly Father, but they always end with the words "through Christ Our Lord. Amen."

Let us Pray

Heavenly Father, we thank you for the gift of faith.
Open to us the power of your Word and your Spirit,
so that our faith may be renewed,
our lives may be transformed,
our gifts may be shared and your kingdom come,
through Christ our Lord. Amen.

What will prayer do for me?

If we open our lives to God in the sacraments and in our daily prayer, we shall find that our whole view of life gradually changes and we begin to see things more from God's point of view.

We cope better with life's problems because we know for certain that we are in God's loving hands. This is a consolation when we are afraid or anxious. We need strong faith and trust, the kind that Mary showed when told that she would be the mother of the Redeemer. It gives us strength to persevere because God knows what he is about. Prayer really does help us to put things in perspective.

Prayer also helps us become more aware of the false values that surround us - the greed, selfishness and self indulgence, the unhappiness and suffering of others and the many injustices in our society. We also become more aware of the immense goodness of many people. The Holy Spirit helps us to judge wisely the things that really matter and choose a path through life that will lead us to God.

Does prayer make God change his mind?

When Jesus was in the Garden of Gethsemane before his arrest, he prayed in great distress:

"My Father, if it is possible, let this cup pass from me; yet not what I want but what you want." (Matthew 26.39)

This is the way we should always pray. Our Lord tells us to ask for what we need, but only if it is God's will. When we ask for help in our troubles, God will either influence the outcome, help us to find a resolution or give us the patience and resignation to cope with the situation. God will never abandon us.

"O God, you are my God, for you I long; for you my soul is thirsting." (Psalm 62)

prayer ... Jesus teaches us about prayer

Jesus teaches us how to pray

Jesus gave clear and simple advice about prayer:

"Whenever you pray, go into your room and shut the door and pray to your Father in secret; and your Father who sees you in secret will reward you....do not heap up empty phrases ... your Father knows what you need before you ask him." (Matthew 6.6 - 8)

Many times in the Gospels we read of Jesus taking time out to pray. Jesus is fully God and fully man. He needed to pray as much as we do, especially at key periods of his life, for example at his baptism:

> "Now when all the people were baptized, and when Jesus had been baptized and was praying, the heaven was opened, and the Holy Spirit descended upon him in bodily form like a dove."
> (Luke 3.21 - 22)

Notice here that the Holy Spirit came upon Jesus to confirm him in his earthly mission as he was at prayer. The same Holy Spirit also came upon the apostles as they too waited in prayer.

Another occasion when Jesus felt the need to pray was before he chose the twelve apostles;

> "Now during those days he went out to the mountain to pray; and he spent the night in prayer to God. And when day came, he called his disciples and chose twelve of them, whom he called apostles." (Luke 6.12 - 13)

On many occasions, Jesus took his disciples apart to rest and pray in a quiet place. Often when he cured the sick he would pray and lay hands on them. His prayer in the Garden of Gethsemane clearly shows how much Jesus needed to pray when he was in such distress. The model of all our prayer is the one prayer which Jesus himself gave us at the request of his disciples - the Our Father.

The Sermon on the Mount

St Matthew describes how Jesus, early in his public ministry, goes up the mountain side to preach. As the crowds gather round he delivers his new manifesto of the Kingdom of God. Matthew presents Jesus as the new Moses, giving the chosen people a new Covenant to live by. This new Covenant goes much deeper than the earlier covenants. As Jesus said, the new Covenant completes and brings to perfection the covenant given to Moses. The new Covenant of the Kingdom of God challenges our whole attitude to life. Jesus turns upside down many of the values by which people live. The harsh justice of God is now tempered by his gentle and forgiving mercy.

- Jesus rejects the worldly values of power, prosperity and comfort.

- Jesus stresses the importance of love and concern for our neighbour.

- Jesus shows us that our obedience is to a person not to an abstract law - e.g. "If you love me, keep my commandments."

The Eight Beatitudes

Jesus later explained what he meant about the Kingdom of God by telling stories (called parables) from everyday life that contain a religious message or truth. But first, Matthew introduces this new teaching about the kingdom with eight statements we now call beatitudes:

1) "Blessed are the poor in spirit, for theirs is the kingdom of heaven.

2) Blessed are those who mourn, for they will be comforted.

3) Blessed are the meek, for they will inherit the earth.

4) Blessed are those who hunger and thirst for righteousness, for they will be filled.

5) Blessed are the merciful, for they will receive mercy.

6) Blessed are the pure in heart, for they will see God.

7) Blessed are the peacemakers, for they will be called children of God.

8) Blessed are those who are persecuted for righteousness' sake, for theirs is the kingdom of heaven." (Matthew 5.3-10)

prayer ... finding a way that helps us

Vocal Prayer

Vocal prayer is when we use words. Most Catholics learn their first vocal prayers at home when they are very young. These would be devotional prayers said at night and morning, before and after meals and for special intentions. The sign of the cross, the Our Father, Hail Mary and Glory be to the Father form the basis of our vocal prayers. Vocal prayer is always valuable; it can be a great support and consolation to pray together with others; the Rosary is the most popular vocal prayer.

Mental Prayer

It may take quite some time for us to find a way to pray that suits us and that we find helpful. We need to persevere in our search as the Holy Spirit guides us to a clearer awarenes of ourselves and of his presence within us. There are many types of mental prayer, or meditation. Over the centuries, different religions and cultures have developed their own techniques which they have found helpful when they come before God in prayer. As we persevere in prayer, we may find that we move from one form of prayer to another.

Lectio (Latin for *Reading*)

One of the simplest forms of mental prayer involves a slow and reflective reading of a passage from the Bible or other religious book - a kind of prayerful spiritual reading. We may then draw from this a resolution for action in our lives, perhaps to try and change our attitude or behaviour in some way. This type of prayer, sometimes called Lectio Divina, has been popular with monastic communities for hundreds of years.

Contemplation

The aim of all prayer is union with God. The more we give time to prayer the sooner we realise that words are not important. If we can empty our minds and imaginations of daily concerns and just remain quiet in the stillness of God's love we are using a form of prayer called Contemplation. This is similar to a method known as Centring Prayer. The basic idea is simple:

a) Sit or kneel comfortably; close your eyes and be aware of your surroundings and then of the presence of God within you.

b) Keep your mind attentive and deal with distractions calmly, offering your concerns to God and repeating a short prayer such as the Holy Name or an invocation like 'Come Holy Spirit.'

c) Bring your prayer time calmly to a close by saying slowly the Our Father.

Unanswered Prayer

What happens when we storm heaven with prayer for a special intention and get no response? God knows what is best for us, but we do not; it can be very difficult at times to believe and trust in God's love. Jesus himself assures us that there is no such thing as an unanswered prayer:

> "So I say to you, ask and it will be given you, search and you will find; knock and the door will be opened for you." (Luke 11.9)

But that does not mean that we will always receive what we ask for. We may have to wait a very long time and even then our prayers may be answered by grief and disappointment. When life is tough and our faith seems to be at a low ebb, we just need to ask Our Lord to renew our faith and give us courage to persevere and trust in his merciful love. Later, when the storm has passed, we can look back and see that things worked out for the best after all. At the end of the day it is an arrogant presumption on our part to expect God's plan for our happiness always to fit in with our own short-sighted ideas. God loves us far too much to let that happen!

For long standing problems - try kneeling.

prayer ... making a difference to my life

Prayer is ...

a way of life;
living in the presence of God;
praising, thanking, asking God;
listening for the voice of God;
waiting on God in faith and trust;

saying YES to God;
knowing God is with you;
never wasted;
always heard;
being silent! adoring! rejoicing!

Suggestions you may find helpful

The busier you are, the more you need to pray.

Make time for prayer; do not just 'fit it in'.

Try to have a routine for prayer; discipline helps us all.

Always try to complete the time you give to prayer.

Begin and end each day with prayer.

Find a quiet place, or find silence within yourself - anywhere.

Calm down; breathe deeply; slowly; and relax!

Make the sign of the cross with reverence and faith.

Place yourself consciously in the presence of God.

Praise and thank God for everything in your life.

Be open to the Holy Spirit; be still before God.

Bring your distractions to God. He knows them already.

God is closer to you than your breath.

In times of dryness, boredom, depression - persevere.

When prayer is a struggle, just say slowly the Our Father.

Worried about tomorrow? God is already there.

Do not just say prayers; BE a prayerful person.

You can pray ...

You can pray with words or with a sigh in your heart.

You can pray aloud with others or silently alone.

You can pray anywhere and at any time, day or night.

You can say prayers from a book or make up your own.

You can pray with tears of joy or tears of grief.

You can beg God for help or thank him for his care.

You can pray for hours or just a few seconds.

You can pray for others or for yourself.

You can offer the greatest prayer at Mass.

You can pray before the Blessed Sacrament.

Miracles happen when you pray.

Miracles happen every day.

and finally ...

Everyday life is the raw material of prayer.

Prayer is caught not taught.

To want to pray is a prayer.

Learning anything important is tiring - prayer included.

Silence between friends is never embarrassing.

God loves us not because we are good.

We are good because God loves us.

Pray not that God will change his mind.

Pray rather that God will change your mind.

Religious Devotions
Our faith is a personal relationship with Jesus Christ. Religious devotions (called sacramentals) can deepen our faith and help us become more aware of the presence of God in our daily lives.

Family Prayer
Bringing the whole family together at the end of the day can be a precious time for everyone, especially for the younger members. A short Gospel passage could be read from the next Sunday's Mass or a decade of the rosary recited for family needs, with everyone able to add their special prayers. Children should be encouraged to follow the Mass with a prayer book or missal appropriate to their age. This helps to avoid distractions and is useful for prayer after Holy Communion. Grace before and after meals, when we ask God's blessing on our food and give thanks at the end, is a valuable means of keeping the starving of the world before our minds. These are just some of the ways in which parents can hand on the Faith to their children.

Morning and Night Prayer
"Wake up on your knees!" is good advice. The best way to begin each day is to rise promptly and commend our day to God with a morning offering prayer. At bed-time we should also kneel, examine our conscience, ask pardon for our sins and thank God for the day's blessings.

The Crucifix and other images
A Catholic home should never be ashamed to display a crucifix or other religious symbol. (e.g. a small picture or statue of Our Lady). The poor quality of much religious art should not deter us from finding a worthy sign of our faith.

Holy Water
It is good to have some holy water in the home to use either when blessing the family or asking God's protection before a journey. Some parents keep holy water in the bedroom for use at night prayers.

Fasting before Mass
As a sign of reverence, we are required to fast from all food and drink, except for water and necessary medicines, for one hour before receiving Holy Communion. (An earlier pious custom, now rarely followed, was to break our fast after Mass with a drink of water before eating.)

Adore, Be Silent, Rejoice!" (Blessed Antonio Rosmini.)

the Our Father - the prayer
our saviour gave us (CCC2759 - 2865)

"The Our Father is the prayer of the Church; it sums up the whole Gospel." (CCC 2761)

Our Father, who art in heaven, hallowed be thy name;
thy kingdom come; thy will be done on earth as it is in heaven.
Give us this day our daily bread; and forgive us our trespasses
as we forgive those who trespass against us;
and lead us not into temptation, but deliver us from evil. Amen.

The Prayer our Saviour gave us
Rabbis were expected to teach their disciples how to pray; so when Jesus was speaking about prayer during the sermon on the mount (Matthew 5.1-7,28) he gave us this most familiar of all Christian prayers. Our Lord may have modelled this prayer on one that was familiar from his worship in the Jewish synagogue. The Our Father is recited in every Mass as a preparation for Holy Communion. It is also used in the Rosary and other devotions. There are two versions of the prayer and we use the longer one found in Matthew (6.9-13). The shorter version is found in St Luke's Gospel (11.2-4).

The name of God
When the Israelites spoke about Almighty God, they used the name *YAWEH* "I am who I am." This is the name which God had given to Moses at Mount Sinai when Moses asked the name of the person who was speaking to him. (Exodus 3.14) Later, this divine name was considered too sacred even to pronounce, so Hebrew reverence substituted the word *ADONAI* ("my Lord"). The Greek translation of this word is Kyrios - Lord.

The Kingdom of God
The Jewish understanding of the "Kingdom of God" looked forward to the end of time when the whole of creation will worship God as Lord of the universe.

"Our Father"
Jesus may well have surprised his listeners when, instead of addressing God by the traditional title *elohim* or *adonai*, he uses the Aramaic word *ABBA*. This Hebrew dialect word means "loving Father"; its modern equivalent would be "Dad", the name that even grown up children use within the family. Our Lord reassures us that God is our loving Father, our friend who cares for us; someone to whom we can turn with trust and confidence. God is always close to us; he loves us all equally and protects and provides for us all. As the Sunday preface reminds us, "In you we live and move and have our being."

"who art in heaven"
Some expressions, like *the gates of heaven* or the *pearly gates* may suggest that we think of heaven as somewhere out in space. But these metaphors are just ways of speaking about heaven and are not meant to be taken literally. Paradise is the presence of God, where we meet God. It is a state of existence, our eternal destiny and true home. When people have a brief moment of utter peace, happiness and contentment they can be deeply aware of the closeness of Almighty God. They may describe the experience as a brief glimpse of heaven. Jesus often speaks about his heavenly Father:

> "Look at the birds of the air; they neither sow nor reap nor gather into barns and yet your heavenly Father feeds them." (Matthew 6.26)

> "No one has ever seen God. It is the only Son who is close to the Father's heart, who has made him known." (John 1.18)

1st Petition:
"Hallowed be thy name"
To *hallow* means to honour and recognize something as holy. The name of God is sacred and here we ask that we may always reverence the name of God, our loving creator, ruler of the world. We give glory to God when we ask the Holy Spirit to help us follow the way Jesus has shown us:

> "Be perfect as your heavenly Father is perfect."

At the Last Supper, Jesus prays to his heavenly Father:

> "I have made your name known to those whom you gave me from the world." (John 17.6)

2nd Petition:
"Thy Kingdom come"
The Kingdom is our own personal relationship with God. Jesus teaches us about the Kingdom in a series of parables; these are simple stories that show how God's lordship of creation will reach its climax at the end of time, and how it has already begun and is at work within each one of us. The Kingdom is like a tiny mustard seed that grows to a great bush, or a hidden treasure, or a valuable pearl for which we sacrifice everything to buy, or a little yeast that leavens all the dough. Jesus told Pilate:

> My Kingdom is not from this world." (John 18.36) St Paul adds:

> "The Kingdom of God is not food and drink but righteousness and peace and joy in the Holy Spirit." (Romans 14.17)

"It is better to say one Our Father fervently than a thousand with no devotion." (St Edmund)

the Our Father
the lord's prayer

3rd Petition: "Thy will be done on earth as it is in heaven."

We pray that we may be faithful to what God asks of us. Jesus came on earth not to do his own will but to do the will of his Heavenly Father. In the Garden of Gethsemane he accepted his Heavenly Father's plan for our salvation and freely gave himself up to his captors. Mary's life was spent in doing God's will. God's will for us is woven into the very fabric of our lives. Prayer helps us see more clearly what God wants of us and also helps us to accept God's will, especially if this involves suffering, grief or loneliness.

4th Petition: "Give us this day our daily bread"

We are reminded that everything is a gift from our Heavenly Father. We are not to worry unduly about our needs (Matthew 6.25), but pray that God will watch over us all. At the same time we remember that we have a responsibility to work for the things we pray for. Our prayers for our starving brothers and sisters must be joined with realistic help for them. When Jesus was tempted in the wilderness he said:

> "One does not live on bread alone, but on every word that comes from the mouth of God." (Matthew 4,4)

Our need of nourishment is not just a physical hunger and thirst, it is also a spiritual yearning for God. We are nourished by the Word of God in the scriptures and by Food from Heaven in the Eucharist.

5th Petition: "Forgive us our trespasses as we forgive those who trespass against us"

We all have feet of clay; we are sinners in need of forgiveness and healing. If we ourselves wish to be forgiven we must first forgive others. Jesus calls us to forgive others:

> "Not seven times, I tell you, but seventy-seven times."
>
> (Matthew 18.22)
>
> "For if you forgive others their trespasses, your heavenly Father will also forgive you; but if you do not ... neither will your Father forgive your trespasses."
>
> (Matthew 6.14 - 15)
>
> "You have heard it said 'You shall love your neighbour and hate your enemy.' But I say to you, love your enemies and pray for those who persecute you."
>
> (Matthew 5.43 - 44)

6th Petition: "And lead us not into temptation"

The world is good, but we can spoil it by selfishness and greed. The way we cope with temptation helps us to understand more about ourselves, what makes us tick. We are free to reject evil and to follow God's law of love, or we can reject it and choose evil instead. Jesus also was tempted - in the wilderness and in Gethsemane. Saint Paul adds a timely word of caution:

> "So if you think you are standing, watch out that you do not fall. ... God is faithful, and he will not let you be tempted beyond your strength, but with the testing he will also provide the way out so that you may be able to endure it." (1Corinthians 10.13)

During his lonely vigil in Gethsemane, Jesus said to Simon Peter:

> "Simon, are you asleep? Could you not keep awake one hour? Keep awake and pray that you may not come into the time of trial; the spirit indeed is willing but the flesh is weak." (Mark 14.37 - 38)

7th Petition: "But deliver us from evil."

At the Last Supper, Jesus prayed that Satan would not overwhelm his disciples:

> "Holy Father, protect them in your name ...I am not asking you to take them out of this world, but I ask you to protect them from the evil one." (John 17.11,15)

We pray here that we will persevere in our faith despite our many daily failings and the evil in the world around us. If our life is marked by failure or suffering, worry, loneliness or distress, we need to trust in God's loving mercy and ask for the grace to carry our cross with peace and joy in our hearts.

"For the kingdom, the power and the glory are yours, now and for ever."
These words are not found in the Gospel account of the Our Father. They first appeared in an early 2nd century collection of Christian prayers called the Didache or *Teaching of the Twelve Apostles*. The Didache added this devotional prayer to the end of the Our Father.

While Martin Luther was in prison in 1521, he translated the New Testament into German, and he used the Didache version of the Lord's Prayer. Since that time it has remained the standard version of the Our Father that is used in Protestant/Anglican/non Catholic churches.

The prayer is included in the Mass as a response to the priest's prayer that follows the Our Father.

(This short addition to the Our Father is an example of a short prayer of praise of God called a *doxology*. Another example of a doxology is the Glory be to the Father prayer.)

Mary mother of God
Mother of the Church

Let us Pray

Hail Mary, full of grace, the Lord is with thee,
Blessed art thou among women,
and blessed is the fruit of thy womb, Jesus.
Holy Mary, Mother of God,
pray for us sinners,
now and at the hour of our death. Amen.

Devotion to Our Blessed Lady

Most Catholics have a special devotion to Our Lady. Mary obeyed God's will in faith and humility; she agreed to become the mother of Jesus. When the angel Gabriel told her what was to happen, Mary said:

"Here I am, the servant of the Lord; let it be with me according to your word." (Luke 1.38)

Almighty God took human nature from Mary; Jesus was conceived by the power of the Holy Spirit.

Why is Mary called the "Mother of God"?

Jesus is both truly God and truly man. He has a human nature like ours and he also has the divine nature of Almighty God. Mary gave birth to Jesus - who is both human and divine. Early in the fifth century, Archbishop Nestorius of Constantinople (Istanbul) said that Mary could only have been the mother of the human nature of Jesus; she could not possibly be given the title of *Mother of God*. In A.D.431 a special meeting was held at Ephesus. At this council the assembled bishops said that there is only one divine person in Jesus and Mary gave birth to him. It follows that we can truthfully say that Mary can be called *Mother of God*.

Mary, Mother of the Church

We are followers of Christ and members of his Church. The second Vatican Council's 1963 document on *The Church* includes a whole chapter on Our Lady which speaks about her role as our model and guide. Mary gave birth to the Son of God, Jesus Christ. Sometimes she is also spoken of as *Mother of the Church*. This is an ancient title and although it was not used in the document on *The Church*, it was used again in 1964 by Pope Paul VI in his closing speech of the Council. The title means that Mary is the perfect example of what all Christians should be - united to Christ in loving obedience to the will of God. When we pray to Mary we use several different titles. These include *Blessed Virgin Mary*, *Our Blessed Lady*, *The Immaculate Conception*, and *Mother of God*.

Mary is our Mother

When Jesus was crucified, Mary, with a few friends including Saint John, remained at the foot of the cross to keep Jesus company in his last agony. Before he died, Jesus gave Mary to us as our mother:

"'Woman, here is your son.' Then he said to the disciple, 'here is your mother.'" (John 19.26 - 27)

Mary will bring us closer to her Divine Son. As we prepare for the gift of the Holy Spirit to strengthen us at Confirmation, let us ask Mary to help us be faithful to the way of life Jesus has shown us. We should pray every day to Our Lady. She will never let us down.

"Mary is a model of the Church in faith, charity and union with Christ." (L.G. No 63)

virgin birth
immaculate conception
pilgrimages

The Virgin Birth

The Virgin Birth means that Jesus did not have a human father. He was conceived by Mary without male intervention. Mary and Joseph were engaged but they were not yet living together as man and wife. So when Mary enquired of the Angel how she, as a virgin, could become a mother, she was told:

" The Holy Spirit will come upon you and the power of the Most High will overshadow you; therefore the child to be born will be holy; he will be called Son of the Most High."
(Luke 1.35)

The Gospel accounts of the conception and birth of Jesus in Matthew and Luke date from about A.D.80. Both clearly state that Jesus was conceived by the power of the Holy Spirit; and they stress this by the names they use; *Jesus (God saves), Messiah, Saviour, Emmanuel, God with us, Son of the Most High, Holy One of God, Descendant of David.*

The Immaculate Conception

The title *The Immaculate Conception* means that God kept Mary free from sin from the first moment of her existence and untouched by the original sin in which we are born. Mary was filled with the love of God. That is why we pray to her: "Hail Mary, full of grace."

Christians have long accepted (in England since the 11th century) that it was appropriate for Mary to have been preserved from sin in view of her role in God's plan for the salvation of the world. On December 8th 1854, Pope Pius IX stated that Mary's Immaculate Conception was part of the Church's official teaching: "The Blessed Virgin Mary, from the first moment of her conception, by the singular grace and privilege of Almighty God and in view of the merits of Jesus Christ, the Saviour of the human race, was preserved free from all stain of original sin."

Why go on pilgrimage?

A pilgrimage is a journey to a shrine of a saint or place of religious importance. Hazardous in medieval times and undertaken as penance for sin, nowadays the physical journey to an unfamiliar destination is symbolic of our journey through life and of our own inner search for a deeper relationship with God and a better knowledge of ourselves.

The shared experience of foreign travel is a chance to deepen our faith and enjoy the company of new friends. The weariness of long journeys, unfamiliar language, diet and customs are all part of the pilgrimage experience. Most return spiritually refreshed, physically weary maybe, but richer in faith, if not in pocket. They know it has been worth while.

Shrines of Our Lady

Shrines are places of pilgrimage and prayer. Popular throughout Europe in medieval times, there are still well established shrines in honour of Our Lady throughout the U.K. Rome and the Holy Land have always been the main pilgrimage destinations. But in addition to Lourdes, there are many other popular shrines of Our Lady in Italy, Poland, Portugal and since 1981, Medjugorje in Yugoslavia, in America, Canada and Mexico. There are also national shrines of Our Lady in these islands: Walsingham in England, Carfin in Scotland, Cardigan in Wales and Knock in the Republic of Ireland.

Lourdes

Lourdes in southern France is the most popular shrine of Our Lady and an important place of Christian pilgrimage. In February 1858 Our Lady appeared several times to a young girl called Bernadette Soubirous and asked her to have a chapel built so that people could come and pray and do penance for their sins. When Bernadette asked the lady's name, Mary replied, "I am the Immaculate Conception." This feast is kept on December 8th.

Since the time of Mary's apparitions, Lourdes has continued to grow in popularity as a place of pilgrimage, with over two million visitors each year. Several large churches have been built on the site to accommodate the pilgrims, very many of whom are sick. Numerous cures have been associated with the healing waters of the spring. This has flowed since the day Bernadette was told by Our Lady to wash in the water at the foot of the rock of apparition.

Popular devotions in honour of Our Lady are part of any pilgrimage to Marian shrines. However, the main focus of faith and devotion at all shrines of Our Lady, is the Sacrifice of the Mass and the Real Presence of Our Lord in the Blessed Sacrament. Pilgrims attend Mass in great numbers and spend many hours in adoration before the Blessed Sacrament. This is consistent with Mary's mission - to bring us to her Divine Son. Most Catholics believe the apparitions of Our Lady to be genuine and many of the cures to be miraculous, but they are not an essential part of Catholic teaching.

Mary, conceived without sin, pray for us who have recourse to thee.

the rosary

The Rosary

This popular prayer to Our Lady takes its name from the Latin word *rosarium* which means a rose garden. In medieval times, the rose was seen as a symbol of eternal life. The title 'Mystical Rose' is one of the invocations in the Litany of Our Lady. Mary was the first person to be redeemed by Christ.

A rosary, sometimes called 'rosary beads' or even a 'set of beads', is simply a string of beads (or a finger ring of beads) that we use to keep track of the number of prayers we have said. The idea is very ancient indeed and has been common practice since well before the time of Christ in many parts of the world. The prayer beads can be as simple as a piece of knotted string.

What is a Litany?

A Litany is a series of short recited or sung petitions with a response or reply that is repeated after each invocation. Litanies in honour of the Sacred Heart and Our Lady have been a part of popular devotions in some countries for many years. The Litany of Our Lady is sometimes said or sung after the public recitation of the Rosary. It is also called the Litany of Loreto after the name of the popular Italian shrine of Our Lady near Ancona on the Adriatic Coast.

Do Catholics worship Mary?

Catholics do not worship Mary and have never done so. Worship belongs to God alone. However, some people think that Catholics give too much attention to Our Blessed Lady. The Second Vatican Council document on *The Church - Light of the Nations* reminds us that Mary, like all the human race, was saved by Christ, and warns against exaggerated devotions that can distort the truth. We reverence Mary as a human being who has reached the highest state of union with God. She is our model and exemplar, a woman of humble faith and loving obedience. Her powerful intercession comes from her unique role as mother of our Redeemer.

What is a Rosary?

A rosary consists of five groups of ten beads called decades which are separated by a single larger bead. The Our Father is recited on the larger bead and ten Hail Mary's on the smaller ones. At the end of each decade the Glory be to the Father is said on the large bead which is then used for the Our Father for the beginning of the following decade.

The complete rosary now consists of four sets of these five decades. Each set focuses on different events, called mysteries, in the life of Our Lord. These are called the *Joyful,* the *Sorrowful,* the *Glorious* and the *Luminous* mysteries (or *Mysteries of Light*). The Mysteries of Light were added to the rosary by Pope John Paul II in 2002 and they reflect on five incidents in Our Lord's public ministry.

How do I pray the Rosary?

Most people get distracted when they try to pray and find it difficult to keep their minds on what they are doing, especially when saying the rosary. Pope John Paul II suggested that one way of keeping our minds focused when we pray the rosary is to read the Gospel passage that mentions the particular event or mystery we are about to say. Then we can pause for a few moments and think about the Gospel event before we begin each decade. We can also offer up each decade for a particular intention and we can either reflect on the Gospel event as we say the Hail Mary's or concentrate on the meaning of the words we are saying.

We should not be surprised or depressed when distractions crowd into our minds; they are all part of life's concerns and we can offer them all to God when we become aware of them. Some people just say one decade at a time and return to complete the prayer at different moments during the day.

When did the Rosary first become popular?

The Hail Mary was probably in use by the 6th century in the eastern Church and it was firmly established in western Christendom by the 11th century. One popular devotion was to say 150 Our Fathers, called *Paternosters,* instead of reciting the 150 psalms. London's Paternoster Row was famous for its rosary makers.

In medieval times, when people recited the psalms and devotional prayers, they would sometimes link them to a Gospel verse about Our Lady. Gradually a separate devotion developed in honour of Mary. Short, prayerful reflections based on references to her in the Gospel were followed by a number of Hail Mary's.

In the 13th century both Saint Dominic and Saint Francis encouraged people to pray the rosary in honour of Our Lady and by the 16th century it had assumed its present form. The Christian naval victory over the Turks at Lepanto in 1571 was attributed to the intercession of Our Blessed Lady. In 1577, the Dominican Pope Pius V established the feast day of Our Lady of the Rosary.

"The Rosary is a prayer for the family." (Pope John Paul II RVM No.41)

the mysteries of the rosary

The Joyful Mysteries (said on Monday and Saturday)

1) The Annunciation (Luke 1.30 - 32)
"The angel said to her, 'Do not be afraid, Mary, for you have found favour with God. And now you will conceive in your womb and bear a son, and you will name him Jesus. He will be great and will be called Son of the Most High.'"

2) The Visitation (Luke 1.41 - 42)
"When Elizabeth heard Mary's greeting, the child leaped in her womb. And Elizabeth was filled with the Holy Spirit and exclaimed with a loud cry, 'Blessed are you among women and blessed is the fruit of your womb.'"

3) The Birth of Our Lord (Luke 2.7)
"And she gave birth to her first born son, wrapped him in swaddling clothes and laid him in a manger, because there was no room for them in the inn."

4) The Presentation in the Temple (Luke 2.22, 28 - 32)
"They brought him up to Jerusalem to present him to the Lord...Simeon took him in his arms and praised God, saying, 'Master, now you are dismissing your servant in peace ... my eyes have seen your salvation ...a light for revelation to the Gentiles and for glory to your people Israel.'"

5) The Finding in the Temple (Luke 2.46 - 47)
"After three days they found him in the temple, sitting among the teachers, listening to them and asking them questions. And all who heard him were amazed at his understanding and his answers."

The Mysteries of Light (said on Thursday)

1) Jesus is baptized in the Jordan (Mark 1.9, 11)
"Jesus came from Nazareth in Galilee and was baptized by John in the Jordan ... And a voice came from heaven, 'You are my Son, the beloved; with you I am well pleased.'"

2) The Manifestation of Jesus at the wedding in Cana
"Jesus said to them, 'Fill the jars with water ... Now draw some out and take it to the chief steward.' Jesus did this, the first of his signs, in Cana of Galilee, and revealed his glory; and his disciples believed in him." (John 2.7 - 11)

3) Proclamation of the Kingdom and call to repentance
"After John was arrested, Jesus came to Galilee, proclaiming the good news of God, and saying, 'The time is fulfilled, and the kingdom of God has come near; repent and believe in the good news.'" (Mark 1.14 - 15)

4) The Transfiguration (Mark 9.2 - 3)
"Jesus took with him Peter and James and John, and led them up a high mountain apart, by themselves. And he was transfigured before them, and his clothes became dazzling white, such as no one on earth could bleach them."

5) The Last Supper and the Institution of the Eucharist
"While they were eating, Jesus took a loaf of bread, and after blessing it he broke it and gave it to the disciples and said, 'Take, eat; this is my body.' Then he took a cup, and after giving thanks he gave it to them, saying, 'Drink from it, all of you; for this is my blood of the covenant.'" (Matthew 26.26 - 28)

The Sorrowful Mysteries (said on Tuesday and Friday)

1) The Agony in the Garden (Luke 22.41 -44)
"Then he withdrew from them about a stone's throw, knelt down and prayed, 'Father, if you are willing, remove this cup from me; yet, not my will but yours be done' ... In his anguish he prayed more earnestly, and his sweat became like great drops of blood falling down on the ground."

2) The Scourging at the Pillar (Mark 15.15)
"So Pilate, wishing to satisfy the crowd, released Barabbas for them; and after flogging Jesus, he handed him over to be crucified."

3) The Crowning with Thorns (Matthew 27.29)
"And after twisting some thorns into a crown, they put it on his head. They put a reed in his right hand and knelt before him, saying, 'Hail, King of the Jews!'"

4) The Carrying of the Cross (John 19.16 -17)
"Then Pilate handed him over to be crucified. So they took Jesus; and carrying the cross by himself, he went out to what is called the Place of the Skull."

5) The Crucifixion (John 19.18 - 30)
"There they crucified him, and with him two others, one on either side with Jesus between them ... When Jesus had received the wine, he said, 'It is finished.' Then he bowed his head and gave up his spirit."

The Glorious Mysteries (Wednesday and Sunday)

1) The Resurrection (Mark 16.9)
"On the first day of the week, he appeared first to Mary Magdalene, from whom he had cast out seven demons."

2) The Ascension (Luke 24.50 - 51)
"He led them out as far as Bethany, and lifting up his hands, he blessed them. While he was blessing them, he withdrew from them and was carried up to heaven."

3) The Descent of the Holy Spirit upon the Apostles
"And suddenly from heaven there came a sound like the rush of a violent wind, and filled the entire house where they were sitting. Divided tongues, as of fire, appeared among them, and a tongue rested on each of them. All were filled with the Holy Spirit and began to speak in other languages, as the Spirit gave them ability." (Acts 2.2 - 4)

4) The Assumption of Our Lady into Heaven
"Just as Christ was raised from the dead by the glory of the Father, so we too might walk in newness of life ...For if we have been united with him in a death like his, we will certainly be united with him in a resurrection like his." (Romans 6.4 - 5)

5) The Crowning of Our Lady as Queen of Heaven
"A great sign appeared in heaven: a woman clothed with the sun, with the moon under her feet, and on her head a crown of twelve stars." (Book of Revelation 12.1)

"The Rosary leads to an encounter with Christ." (Pope John Paul II RVM No.41)

holy week
passion (palm) sunday
the conspiracy begins

The day after his arrest in Gethsemane, Jesus was crucified on Calvary. In that short period he had been questioned five times by four different authorities, accused before the Jewish Council, by witnesses who contradicted themselves, and sentenced to death by a judge who was convinced of his innocence. So the greatest of human crimes became the greatest of heavenly blessings. This brief outline highlights the dramatic events that changed the world for ever.

Jesus enters Jerusalem

About 550 B.C. the prophet Zechariah was encouraging the Jewish people as they set about rebuilding their temple. He looked forward to a time of peace for Israel. He said that the future ruler of God's people would enter the city in this way. "Rejoice greatly, O daughter of Zion! ... Lo, your king comes to you; triumphant and victorious is he, humble and riding on a donkey." (Zechariah 9.9) When he entered the city, Jesus was greeted as "Son of David". This was as good as calling him a king. This incident may well have proved crucial when Pilate was deciding on the fate of Jesus.

Jerusalem at Passover

By the time of Our Lord, Passover had become a joyful celebration of liberation from slavery and an expression of Jewish national and religious identity as the people of God. In contrast, Jesus would focus much more on the sacrificial aspect of the Passover meal.

The main Jewish religious festival attracted up to one hundred thousand extra visitors to the city. In addition to the many devout Jewish pilgrims who returned each year to celebrate Passover, there would be Greek-speaking tourists, Syrian traders and an extra large garrison of Roman soldiers to maintain public order in the city. For the Roman authorities, Passover presented the threat of civil unrest, with a potentially explosive mix of large crowds, religious fervour and frustrated nationalism.

Jesus raises Lazarus from the dead

Our story really begins about two weeks before Holy Week, when Jesus begins his journey south from Galilee to celebrate Passover in Jerusalem.

On the way he warns that he will be crucified and will rise again. When he hears that his friend Lazarus is dying, Jesus decides to go to him. John tells us that his disciples try to warn him off; the last time he was in Jerusalem the people tried to stone him for claiming to be the Son of God.

Jesus knows that Lazarus will be dead, but he tells his disciples that it will help them to believe in him. At Bethany, two miles from Jerusalem he greets Lazarus' sisters, Martha and Mary, and raises Lazarus from the dead in front of a startled crowd. Many now believe in him; others, worried about a popular uprising, go to the Pharisees who call a meeting of the Council of chief priests and elders:

> "Caiaphas, who was high priest that year, said to them, 'You know nothing at all! You do not understand that it is better for you to have one man die for the people than to have the whole nation destroyed.'" (John 11.49 - 50)

Meanwhile, Jesus with his disciples leaves the area and spends a few days in Ephraim to prepare for what lies ahead.

Passion (Palm) Sunday

Jesus enters Jerusalem in triumph, riding on a donkey. He is welcomed by a rejoicing crowd who had heard about his raising Lazarus from the tomb.

They acclaim him as king and Messiah. (Matthew 21.9) He enters the temple and with a prophetic and defiant gesture he drives out the money changers and stall holders. The crowds flock to him and he cures the blind and the lame.

His final three days of preaching are disrupted by growing opposition from the Jewish leaders. Jesus denounces the scribes and pharisees; he calls them hypocrites and warns the Apostles that he will soon be arrested and crucified:

> "You know that after two days the Passover is coming, and the Son of Man will be handed over to be crucified. Then the chief priests and the elders of the people gathered in the palace of the high priest, who was called Caiaphas, and they conspired to arrest Jesus by stealth and kill him. But they said, 'Not during the festival, or there may be a riot among the people.'"
> (Matthew 26.2-5)

Their decision was made before Judas came to them. They had only a couple of days in which to get rid of Jesus and his followers. Any delay would allow them all to return to their homes after the feast. Speed and secrecy were essential to avert a public outcry or even a civil riot among the rabble of lower classes who followed Jesus.

"Blessed is the king who comes in the name of the Lord!" (Luke 19.38)

wednesday betrayal
thursday last supper
new commandment

Wednesday -
The meal at Bethany with Lazarus and his sisters

As the festival draws near, Jesus accepts an invitation to eat with Martha and Mary. Mary administers the courtesy perfume offered to guests, but to everyone's amazement, she pours the whole pound of nard, an expensive aromatic oil, over his feet. Judas complains that the perfume could have been sold for three hundred denarii (one year's wages for a labourer) and the money given to the poor. But Saint John tells us that Judas was a thief who stole from the common purse. Jesus stops any criticism by praising her kindness and saying that she has prepared his body for burial.

The word Messiah means 'one who is anointed for the service of God.' Jewish kings were anointed on the head; this gesture of honour and respect may also have been Mary's symbolic recognition of Christ, the Messiah.

Judas may now have realised that Jesus was not going to be the kind of Messiah he had expected and decides to change his allegiance:

"Then one of the twelve, who was called Judas Iscariot, went to the chief priests and said 'What will you give me if I betray him to you?' They paid him thirty pieces of silver. And from that moment he began to look for an opportunity to betray him." (Matthew 26.14-16)

Thursday -
The Last Supper

This was a busy day as preparations were made throughout the city for the Passover celebrations. Jesus asks Peter and John to go up to Jerusalem and prepare the room for their Passover meal. Following Jesus' instructions, they approach a man carrying a pitcher of water (men usually carried water in larger skins) who directs them to the upper room and they prepare the lamb (sacrificed in the temple) for roasting, the unleavened matzos, the salad of bitter herbs, the wine and the bowl of almonds, figs, dates, wine and cinnamon

A new Commandment - love one another

Although Passover is a joyful feast, Jesus is more than usually reflective on this occasion. Saint Luke mentions an argument during the meal about who was the most important member of their group. To everyone's surprise, Jesus suddenly stands up and puts aside his outer garment. He wraps a towel round his waist, pours water into a basin and begins to wash their feet. They are dumbfounded. Jesus ignores Peter's protests and gives a powerful example of loving service of each other. They do not understand; so Jesus explains:

"You call me Teacher and Lord - and you are right, for that is what I am. So, if I, your Lord and Teacher, have washed your feet, you also ought to wash one another's feet. For I have set you an example, that you also should do as I have done to you." (John 13.13 - 15)

Later, when Judas had left the company on his shameful errand, Jesus says:

Just as I have loved you, you also should love one another. By this everyone will know that you are my disciples, if you have love for one another." (John 13.34 - 35)

Good Works
The rabbis identified two grades of 'good works' - almsgiving was the basic grade but the higher grade included burying the dead and preparing a body for burial. It was to this corporal work of mercy that Jesus was referring in his reply to the critics. The perfume used by Mary is described as 'pure Nard' by Saint Mark. It was known to be expensive because it was extracted from a plant native to India, from where it may have originated.

Jesus shows respect for women
Jesus showed great respect for women. Jewish society at the time of Christ had strict views on the role of women. They led very restricted lives and were generally confined to the house, unless they were obliged to visit the synagogue or market, veiled and accompanied, or to work in the fields. They belonged to their fathers before marriage and to their husbands afterwards. Girls were not educated either at home or in the synagogue. A man could divorce his wife, or take a second one or a concubine (mistress), but divorce was all but impossible for a woman. Jesus was the only rabbi with women disciples and he had several women friends. He taught that men should marry only one woman and be faithful to her for life; he also said that some prostitutes were nearer to God than the religious leaders. Women travelled with him and supported him, and they were the first to witness his resurrection.

Maundy Thursday
Mandatum is Latin for 'commandment' from which we get *MAUNDY*. Jesus washes the apostles' feet to give us an example of his new commandment of love. At the evening Mass of the Lord's Supper on Maundy Thursday, the priest may wash the people's feet. In the Anglican tradition, the word MAUNDY refers to specially minted silver coins (Maundy Money) distributed to the poor by the monarch on this day.

thursday
betrayal by Judas
the first eucharist

Judas the betrayer"

We know little of this sad and disillusioned man, corrupted by greed and ambition. It seems that he was the one member of the twelve who came from Judaea, the rest of the group were from Galilee. His request, "What will you give me if I betray him to you?", says much about his character. The chief priests offer him thirty silver shekels - the forfeit for killing a slave. This may have been a calculated insult on the part of the authorities.

When Judas saw Jesus being tried for his life in front of Pilate, he was overcome with guilt and returned the money to the Sanhedrin saying that he had sinned in betraying an innocent's blood. His tragic end may have reflected his remorse as he inflicted the death penalty on himself. The temple priests, ever concerned about legal niceties, were concerned only with how best to spend this blood money. They bought with it a burial ground for strangers.

Jesus says that he will be betrayed

"Jesus was troubled in spirit, and declared, 'Very truly, I tell you, one of you will betray me.'"
(John 13. 21)

The apostles ask who could do such a thing; and Peter asks John who reclined nearest to Our Lord, to find out who it is,

"Jesus answered, 'It is the one to whom I give this piece of bread when I have dipped it in the dish.' ... he gave it to Judas son of Simon Iscariot. After he received the piece of bread, Satan entered into him. Jesus said to him, 'Do quickly what you are going to do.'"
(John 13.26-27)

Judas leaves the group but not to buy provisions or to give alms to the poor. Jesus' darkest hour will soon be upon him. John makes the chilling comment:

"And it was night." (John 13.30)

Jesus consecrates bread and wine - the first Mass

"While they were eating, Jesus took a loaf of bread, and after blessing it he broke it , gave it to the disciples, and said, 'Take eat: this is my body.' Then he took a cup and after giving thanks he gave it to them, saying, 'Drink from it, all of you, for this is my blood of the covenant, which is poured out for many for the forgiveness of sins.'"
(Matthew 26.26-28)

These words of consecration have been used by the priest at each Mass since the Last Supper. Jesus ordains his first priests when he says:

"Do this in remembrance of me."
(Luke 22.19)

The New Passover Covenant

In these words of consecration, Jesus unites the Passover Feast with his own sacrificial death and resurrection. Jesus is the new Passover victim, the new paschal lamb. So we pass from the old Jewish Covenant to a new,

Christian Covenant, uniting us for ever to our heavenly Father. The death of Jesus makes atonement for our sins and his resurrection makes it possible for him to share his life with us when we are baptized and receive the other sacraments. This awesome reality gradually becomes clear after the Holy Spirit comes upon the Apostles at Pentecost.

Jesus instructs his apostles and prays to his Heavenly Father for them

Saint John records Jesus' long farewell to his friends:

"Do not let your hearts be troubled. Believe in God, believe also in me." "If you love me, you will keep my commandments." "The Advocate, the Holy Spirit, whom the Father will send in my name, will teach you everything and remind you of all that I have said to you." "I am the vine, you are the branches. Those who abide in me and I in them bear much fruit, because apart from me, you can do nothing." "So you have pain now; but I will see you again, and your hearts will rejoice, and no one will take your joy from you."

"Righteous Father, the world does not know you, but I know you; and these have known that you have sent me and have loved them even as you loved me."
(see John chapters 14-17)

"Jesus knew that his hour had come to depart from this world and go to the Father." (John 13.1)

thursday
peter's denial
gethsemane
the arrest of Jesus

Jesus warns Peter that he will soon deny him

The Passover meal in the upper room ends with the final prayers and psalm, and Jesus takes leave of his little band of friends. They are already stunned by his news that one of their number will betray him. But he now tells them that they are all soon to lose faith in him. Peter and the others protest their undying loyalty; but Jesus replies with a stark warning to Peter:

> "Jesus said to him 'Truly I tell you, this day, this very night, before the cock crows twice, you will deny me three times.'" (Matthew 26.34)

And so the joyous Passover atmosphere is tinged with sadness and foreboding.

The apostles have witnessed wondrous things this night. Further mysteries await them, and the full range of emotions - from guilt, grief and paralysing fear to disbelief, ecstatic joy and wonder at the resurrection, and the awesome power of the Holy Spirit at Pentecost. All this in the days and weeks that lie ahead.

The Agony in the Garden of Gethsemane

At about 9.30 p.m. Jesus leaves the upper room and descends the stone steps leading to the Fountain Gate. He crosses the Kidron valley between the city and the Mount of Olives and makes his way to a private olive grove where he sometimes went to pray in peace and quiet.

Jesus enters this familiar retreat with only his closest friends. He is overwhelmed with grief at the horrific ordeal his heavenly Father wishes him to undergo. He knows that his suffering and death will atone for the universal evil of mankind, yet the thought of what awaits him fills him with terror. No wonder it is called the Agony in the Garden. Jesus prays aloud, as was the Jewish custom, and his friends record a few of his anguished prayers:

> "Then he said to them, 'I am deeply grieved, even to death; remain here and stay awake with me.' And going a little further, he threw himself on the ground and prayed, 'My Father, if it is possible, let this cup pass from me; yet not what I want but what you want.'"
> (Matthew 26.38 - 39)

The desolation of Jesus was increased when he realised that, despite begging Peter, James and John to stay awake and keep him company, he found them three times fast asleep, overcome by weariness and grief.

The betrayal and arrest of Jesus

Jesus accepts his Father's will that he should sacrifice his life for the sins of the world. The sound of an approaching crowd announces the arrival of Judas and an armed band from the temple authorities. The disciple Judas greets his rabbi, Jesus, with the customary kiss and identifies him for his captors. Despite this treachery, Jesus still greets Judas with forgiveness and courtesy:

> "Friend, do what you are here to do."
> (Matthew 26.50)

Saint John adds that Jesus shows his power and his voluntary submission:

> "Whom are you looking for?' They answered 'Jesus of Nazareth.' .... When Jesus said to them 'I am he,' they stepped back and fell to the ground."
> (John 18.4 - 6)

Jesus asks why the armed force is needed; he had taught openly in the temple, but he submits to the arrest. During a brief struggle Peter injures a man whom Jesus promptly heals. Jesus is led away into custody and the apostles flee for their lives.

The Kidron valley
The Kidron valley is a steep ravine that separates the temple mount, towering two hundred feet above, from the Mount of Olives. There is a seasonal stream (now housed in a culvert beneath the main road). It is mentioned in 2 Samuel 15.23 when King David (C.1000 B.C) had to flee Jerusalem when faced with a revolt by his son Absalom. He crossed the Kidron brook and made his escape over the Mount of Olives.

Gethsemane
The name comes from the Aramaic for *oilpress*. The present Garden of Gethsemane may not be the exact location of Jesus' vigil before his arrest , but it was certainly in this area, which has been the site of an olive grove for centuries. The present eight olive trees are well over five hundred years old.

Annas

Annas first became High Priest when Jesus was eleven years old. Although he was technically no longer the senior priest, he remained the real power behind the temple priesthood. Five of his family had become High Priests. The Roman Governor Valerius Gratus removed him from office but Annas remained a rich and powerful schemer who ran the temple administration as a private business. His agents exchanged money for the temple coinage at high profits and sold animals for sacrifice. When Jesus was arrested, the high priest was Annas' son-in law, Caiaphas.

The Trial

Strict rules governed trials involving the death penalty. The council of seventy-one members sat in a semicircle with two clerks in front to record the votes for and against the accused. Defence evidence was heard first, followed by the prosecution. The evidence of two witnesses secured a conviction. A simple majority was enough to acquit the accused in which case the verdict could be announced the same day. A guilty verdict had to wait until the following day - as happened to Jesus.

Some aspects of the trial of Jesus were illegal:

a) Jewish law required the witnesses to arrest the accused. Jesus was arrested by temple guards and Roman soldiers.

b) It was illegal to try a capital charge at night.

c) It was illegal for the judge to cross-examine the accused after the evidence of witnesses has broken down.

d) False witnesses were to be stoned.

Other aspects of the trial show more attention to some legal points:

a) Several contradictory witnesses were rejected - showing Caiaphas to be meticulous in following this point of Hebrew legal practice.

b) The first hearing in the house of Caiaphas was irregular. It was necessary to confirm the decision of Caiaphas and the scribes and elders by an official trial hearing during daylight hours within the temple precinct.

c) The guilty verdict was announced the day after Jesus was convicted.

First interrogation of Jesus - by Annas

Annas was not the current High Priest, but Jesus is brought first before him, possibly because he controlled the temple affairs. He questions Jesus about his teaching. Jesus replies:

> "Why do you ask me? Ask those who heard what I said to them; they know what I said."
> (John 18.21)

Jesus is struck across the face and asks why he was so treated. After this brief ordeal he is taken to Annas' son-in-law, Caiaphas, the ruling High Priest.

Second interrogation of Jesus - by Caiaphas

From the different Gospel accounts it seems that there were two sessions of the Sanhedrin court; one late on Thursday night at the home of Caiaphas and the second early on Friday morning in the temple. Three charges were eventually levelled against Jesus:

- ### Jesus had threatened to destroy the temple.

After several failed attempts to incriminate him:

> "At last two came forward and said. ' This fellow said I am able to destroy the temple of God and to build it in three days.'"
> (Matthew 26.61)

This charge of sacrilege was a capital offence, but Mark tells us that the evidence still did not agree properly and was thrown out by the court. Caiaphas was losing control. Time was running out and Jesus was still unconvicted. Any decision of this small court had to be put before the full assembly of the Council the following morning. Caiaphas played his trump card with a second charge:

- ### Jesus is challenged to answer under oath.

Irritated by Jesus refusing to answer the charges, Caiaphas places him under oath to answer or face the charge of blasphemy - and death. He says:

> "'Are you the Messiah, the Son of the Blessed One?' Jesus said , 'I am; and you will see the Son of Man seated at the right hand of the Power and coming with the clouds of heaven.'"
> (Mark 14.61 - 62)

Jesus answered clearly "I am." He uses the reply God gave to Moses when he asked the name of God. Jesus then quotes from the prophecy of Daniel (7.13) and Psalm 110 implying that he is the Messiah King who will come from heaven to rule and judge mankind. Caiaphas tears open the neck of his garment in a ritual gesture of horror at hearing such blasphemy. Jesus has now convicted himself by his confession. Witnesses are no longer necessary; all agree on the penalty of death. With only the formalities of sentencing remaining until the next day, the servants and guards submit Jesus to ridicule, mockery and beatings.

"Caiaphas ... advised the Jews that it was better to have one person die for the people." (John 18. 14)

friday
peter's denial

Jesus before pilate and herod

Peter denies knowing anything about Jesus

A disciple known to Caiaphas brings Peter into the courtyard of the high priest's house. Soldiers and servants gather around an open fire against the chill night air, and Peter joins them, waiting to see what will happen to Jesus. In the light of the flames he is recognised and challenged by a servant girl. Gripped by fear, three times Peter denies with increasing vehemence that he knows anything about the Nazarene, but his accent gives him away.

Eventually the cock crows and Peter comes to his senses. Meanwhile, Jesus is being led through the courtyard; he turns and glances at Peter. Peter remembers the promise he made to Jesus. He rushes out into the night sobbing bitterly. Yet again he has failed his master.

FRIDAY
Third interrogation of Jesus - by Pilate

The Sanhedrin met in the temple early on Friday morning to complete the formalities of condemning Jesus to death for blasphemy. However, aware that Pilate would not execute Jesus for religious opinions and determined to secure Jesus' execution, they introduce their third charge against Jesus, a political one that Pilate could not ignore:

• **Jesus had stirred up the people against Caesar.**

Passover was a public holiday and the courts would be closed for the festival. The only way to secure the death of Jesus before the feast was for Caiaphas to petition Pilate

for a special emergency hearing, early on Friday morning. It seems likely that Caiaphas would have arranged this after he had interrogated Jesus on Thursday night. This late visit may have disturbed Pilate's wife, because shortly after Pilate began hearing Jesus' case the following morning, she sent a message to him:

> "Have nothing to do with that innocent man, for today I have suffered a great deal because of a dream about him."
> (Matthew 27.19)

The chief priests and the band of accusers begin by accusing Jesus of refusing to pay taxes and of claiming to be a king. Pilate takes Jesus inside to speak with him away from the shouting crowd:

> "Pilate asked him, 'So you are a king?' Jesus answered, " You say that I am king. For this I was born ... to testify to the truth. Everyone who belongs to the truth listens to my voice.' Pilate asked him. 'What is truth?'"
> (John 18.37 - 38)

Fourth interrogation of Jesus - by Herod

Pilate returns to face the chief priests and the crowd and tells them that there is no case to answer:

> "I find no basis for an accusation against this man."
> (Luke 23.4)

But the Jews insist that Jesus has been stirring up trouble throughout Judea in the south and Galilee in the north where Jesus was brought up. Pilate sees a way out of the impasse. He sends Jesus under guard to Herod, the governor of Galilee who was in Jerusalem for the feast. The chief priests and scribes join the group to accuse Jesus before Herod. Despite rigorous questioning by Herod, priests and scribes, Jesus remains silent. He is dressed in the scarlet robe of a 'king' and mocked and beaten before being sent back to Pilate.

The cock crow
When Jesus forecasts Peter's three-fold denial, he may have been referring to the Roman bugle call which announced the changing of the guard in the Antonia fortress. This garrison was built overlooking and adjoining the north of the temple area. The third Roman watch from midnight to 3.00 am. was called the *gallicinium* or cock-crow.

The Herod Dynasty
Wherever possible, the Romans preferred indirect rule in their provinces. They used the powerful Edomite family (originally from south of the Dead Sea) to govern Palestine. Herod the Great was king when Jesus was born. He ruled for over thirty years. He was hated by the Jews because he was not Jewish himself and because he collaborated with Rome. He tried to pacify the Jews by marrying Jewish wives and by building the temple in Jerusalem. For the Romans he built the garrison port of Caesarea. He was a ruthless despot who ordered the murder of many children in order to eliminate the danger of a future rival king. His son, Herod Antipas, was ruler when Jesus was sent to him by Pilate. It was he who ordered the execution of John the Baptist.

The Sanhedrin
The Romans respected local native law and law officers in the provinces they controlled. The Sanhedrin was the supreme secular and religious Jewish court and the high priest was the president. Capital sentences were always reserved to the Roman governor. The Sanhedrin or Council comprised seventy-one members, comprising:
Elders: These were the heads of the chief families and clans.
High Priests: These were the current and former high priests and heads of the four high priestly families.
Scribes: These were professional lawyers, most of whom were members of the Pharisee sect.

"Pilate went out to the Jews and told them; 'I find no case against him.'" (John 18.38)

friday
barabbas
pilate condemns Jesus to death

Fifth interrogation of Jesus - by Pilate

Once again Pilate faces the angry crowd:

"I have examined him in your presence and have not found this man guilty of any of your charges against him. Neither had Herod for he sent him back to us. Indeed he has done nothing to deserve death. I will therefore have him flogged and release him."

(Luke 23.14 - 16)

The sight of Jesus, bound, broken by torture, and covered in blood from the flogging and crown of thorns, does little to satisfy the crowd, now roused to a dangerous fury as they clamour for the death of the Son of God.

Pilate tries one more time. He offers a festival amnesty - the release of either Jesus or a convicted murderer called Barabbas. This is rejected. They choose Barabbas and once again demand the death of Jesus.

Pilate condemns Jesus to death by crucifixion

Then the crowd begin to threaten Pilate:

"Everyone who claims to be a king sets himself against the emperor...."

(John 19.12)

Pilate finally surrenders to blackmail in fear of being misrepresented in Rome:

"'Shall I crucify your King?' The chief priests answered, 'We have no king but the emperor.'"

(John 19.15)

"... Pilate saw that he could do nothing, but rather that a riot was beginning, he took some water and washed his hands before the crowd, saying, 'I am innocent of this man's blood; see to it yourselves... So he released Barabbas for them: and after flogging Jesus, he handed him over to be crucified."

(Matthew 27.24 - 26)

Jesus is crucified on Calvary

The Romans reserved crucifixion for the crimes of murder and rebellion. The humiliation of this most painful death robbed the victim of any human dignity. Roped and nailed to the cross, some lingered for days in terrible agony. A peg was sometimes provided to support the body and prolong the torture. Eventually, physical exhaustion, loss of blood or exposure would cause heart failure or asphyxiation.

Jesus shoulders the cross beam for his final journey to the place of execution. The soldiers fear that he might die before reaching Golgotha, so:

"They compelled a passer-by, who was coming in from the country, to carry his cross; it was Simon of Cyrene, the father of Alexander and Rufus."

(Mark 15.21)

His name and crime, written on a board and hung from his neck, is later nailed to the cross above his head. Crucified between two thieves, he pulls himself up to breathe and nails tear on flesh and sinew. Exhausted by scourging, his agony is over within a few hours and he breathes his last.

To hasten the victims' deaths and to dispose of the bodies before the feast, the soldiers break their legs. As Jesus is already dead, a soldier thrusts a spear through his side. Blood and water flow out. Meanwhile, the soldiers in the execution party pass the time by playing dice for the victims' clothes.

"Then Jesus cried again with a loud voice and breathed his last." (Matthew 27.50)

friday
the last words of Jesus
Jesus dies on the cross

The last words of the dying Jesus

From the four Gospel accounts, we have a record of the final words of Our Lord. These are traditionally known as the seven last words of Christ:

1   Jesus prays for the Roman soldiers and for his own people:

" Father, forgive them; for they do not know what they are doing."   (Luke 23.34)

2   A fellow victim beside Jesus curses him and is rebuked by his companion. He asks Jesus to remember him when he comes into his kingdom. Jesus replies:

"Truly I tell you, today you will be with me in Paradise."

3   Saint John remains at the foot of the cross with Mary and her two friends:

"Jesus said to his mother, 'Woman, here is your son.' Then he said to the disciple, 'Here is your mother.' And from that hour the disciple took her into his own home."   (John 19.26 - 27)

4   Jesus then prays Psalm 22, which is a cry for help in time of distress:

"At three o'clock, Jesus cried out with a loud voice, 'My God, my God, why have you forsaken me?'" (Matthew 27.46)

5   "When Jesus knew that all was now finished, ... he said, 'I am thirsty.'"   (John 19.28)

6   "A jar full of sour wine was standing there. So they put a sponge full of wine on a branch of hyssop and held it to his mouth. When Jesus had received the wine, he said, ' It is finished.' Then he bowed his head and gave up the spirit."   (John 19.29 - 30)

7   Saint Luke adds the final words of the dying Son of God:

"Then Jesus, crying with a loud voice, said, 'Father, into your hands I commend my spirit.' Having said this, he breathed his last."   (Luke 23.46)

"Truly this man was God's Son!" (Mark 15.39)

Jesus rises from the dead

On the third day after his death on Calvary, Jesus rises triumphantly from the tomb. For forty days he explains the scriptures to his bewildered disciples. He tells them to wait in Jerusalem for the Holy Spirit to come upon them.

The Tomb of Christ

The tomb in which the body of Jesus had been buried was a private vault built by Joseph of Arimathea. He was a highly respected and influential member of the Sanhedrin. But, unlike the other members of the supreme Jewish tribunal, Joseph was sympathetic towards Jesus and his message. He may well have wanted to honour our Lord in his death even if he had not felt able to speak more forcibly on his behalf while he was still alive. The tomb was a simple stone shelf along one wall of a small, low ceilinged cave, cut out of the hillside. A tiny anteroom led to the single low doorway; old mill stones were sometimes used for this purpose. The corpse was laid on the stone shelf on a long piece of linen which would be drawn up and over the top of the head.

The Resurrection

In the early hours of that Sunday morning as dawn was breaking, four women hurried through the silent streets and alleys of Jerusalem. They were Mary Magdalene, Mary, the wife of Cleopas, Joanna, the wife of Chusa (an official at King Herod's court) and Salome, the wife of Zebedee and mother of the apostles James and John. Their pious intention was to complete the embalming of the corpse of Mary's son, Jesus. (Our Lady is not mentioned. Was she overcome with grief and shock: or did she perhaps suspect or know that her son's body would not be there?)

The empty tomb

Many people saw the empty tomb and the risen Christ, but no one was present as Jesus rose from the dead. All four evangelists tell the same story, with only minor variations. Matthew mentions an earth tremor, the rolling back of the stone and the meeting between Mary Magdalene and Jesus. Luke is very similar to Mark; and John speaks of Peter and himself running to the tomb.

"They had been saying to one another, 'Who will roll away the stone for us from the entrance to the tomb?' When they looked up, they saw that the stone, which was very large, had already been rolled back. As they entered the tomb, they saw a young man, dressed in a white robe ... and they were alarmed. But he said to them, 'Do not be afraid; you are looking for Jesus of Nazareth who was crucified. He has been raised; he is not here. Look, there is the place they laid him. But go, tell his disciples and Peter that he is going ahead of you to Galilee.'"
(Mark.16.3-7)

The Disciples meet the risen Christ

"He appeared first to Mary Magdalene ... She went out and told those who had been with him ... But when they heard that he was alive ... they would not believe it. After this he appeared in another form to two of them ... walking into the country. And they ... told the rest, but they would not believe them. Later he appeared to the eleven ... and upbraided them for their lack of faith and stubbornness, because they had not believed those who saw him after he had risen."
(Mark 16.9-14)

"When it was evening on that day, the first day of the week, and the doors of the house where the disciples had met were locked for fear of the Jews, Jesus came and stood among them and said, 'Peace be with you. As the Father has sent me, so I send you.' ... he breathed on them and said to them, 'Receive the Holy Spirit, if you forgive the sins of any, they are forgiven them; if you retain the sins of any they are retained.'" (John 20.19 - 23)

Jesus invites the sceptical Thomas to touch his wounds.

Thomas is not present when Jesus first appears to the apostles. On his next appearance he invites Thomas to touch the wounds in his hands and side.

"Thomas answered him, 'My Lord and my God.' Jesus said to him, 'Have you believed because you have seen me? Blessed are those who have not seen and yet have come to believe.'" (John 20.28 - 29)

"Why do you look for the living among the dead? He is not here, but has risen." (Luke 24.5)

Jesus joins two disciples on the road to Emmaus

Why did Jesus appear to these two people as they walk from Jerusalem to Emmaus? What lessons can we learn from this story? What is Jesus telling us?

An outline of the Emmaus story

The account of the two disciples meeting the risen Christ on the road to Emmaus is one of the great stories of the world. Before we reflect on it in any detail, we need first to read it again slowly and to listen to it with care. (Luke 24.13-35) Jesus joins the couple as they are discussing the extraordinary things that had happened in the last few hours.

> "He asked them, 'What things?'"
> (Luke 24.19)

He asks them to share their worries. They are amazed that this stranger could be unaware of the recent events in the city with the trial and execution of Jesus. They are broken in spirit, their hopes and dreams shattered. (Saint Luke lays the responsibility for the death of Jesus on the Jewish leaders, not on the whole Jewish people).

> "Oh, how foolish you are and slow of heart to believe all that the prophets have declared! Was it not necessary that the Messiah should suffer these things and then enter into his glory?" (Luke 24.25 - 26)

As they walk along, Jesus explains the scriptures to them; he shows that the cross is part of life. His death on the cross was the will of his Heavenly Father and it has made atonement for our sins. This has been crowned by his glorious resurrection. The travellers may have begun to realise that Jesus could be the Messiah, but it is unlikely that they believed him to be the Son of God.

As they neared the inn, Jesus does not want to impose himself upon their company. God accepts our free will when he invites us to accept him:

> "He walked ahead as if he were going on. But they urged him strongly, saying, 'Stay with us, because it is almost evening and the day is now nearly over.'"
> (Luke 24.28-29)

> "When he was at table with them, he took bread, blessed and broke it, and gave it to them. Then their eyes were opened, and they recognized him; he vanished from their sight."
> (Luke Luke 24.31)

The expression "Their eyes were opened" occurs eight times in the New Testament. It means that people understood something deeper about the teaching of Jesus.

It is just possible that the "vanishing from their sight" was a later addition to the story. After all, there was no further need for Jesus to be visibly present if he was already with them in the Eucharist. However, this in turn presumes that Jesus actually consecrated bread and wine for them; but Luke's account does not say clearly that this is what actually happened. Either way, the breaking of bread by Jesus was an important gesture for the early Christian community as they reflected on the events of the Last Supper and the Lord's command to:

> "Do this in remembrance of me."
> (Luke 22.19)

Who was Saint Luke?
Luke was a physician from Antioch in Syria. Some of the material he uses in his gospel account is based on Saint Mark and other sources. He wrote his Gospel after A.D.70 - because he mentions Our Lord's warning about the coming destruction of the city and temple of Jerusalem which was razed to the ground after terrible slaughter by the Romans in A.D.70. (Luke 21.5-38) Luke was a well educated and cultured man. A master of the Greek language and a gifted storyteller, he was writing for a sophisticated Gentile community who needed convincing that God was still faithful to his chosen people despite the disasters which had overtaken them.

The Gospel of Luke
Luke's Gospel, and his second volume, *Acts of Apostles*, shows us that God is still faithful to his chosen people. God sends his son Jesus to offer a new covenant of salvation that reaches far beyond the original covenant with Israel. This offer is to a new Israel - to the Gentiles, to repentant sinners, to women, to Samaritans, to the ritually unclean, to those on the fringes of respectable society. This was a big challenge to his Jewish listeners as well as to the early Jewish converts to Christianity. Not only is God faithful to the promises he made through the prophets, but, in Jesus, God completes and fulfils the message of the Old Testament. So, the account of Our Lord's birth and early years has many links with Old Testament tradition. Jerusalem has a special importance for Luke. His gospel begins and ends there; the resurrection appearances occur in and around Jerusalem; and in Acts 1.8 we read that the Faith spreads throughout the Roman empire from Jerusalem. Luke describes how Jesus mixed with the poor and the ordinary folk in the street. He writes about the mercy and forgiveness of Jesus and about his call to personal holiness. He writes about the danger of being caught up by material goods, about the misuse of wealth, the respect due to women, the importance of prayer, the joy of serving God and the importance of the Holy Spirit in our lives.

emmaus
the message in the story

Who were the disciples?

Luke's account implies that this apparition took place on Easter Sunday. Early traditions claimed that the two travellers could have been relatives of Our Lord. This would suggest that at least some of his family (the "brethren of Jesus") did accept him as the Messiah. As the disciples set out on their journey, little did they realise that their disappointment and grief were soon to be replaced by surprise and joy when they meet the risen Son of God as he breaks bread for them at the inn.

Light and darkness

The imagery of darkness and light is a constant theme in the Bible. Creation begins with the separation of darkness and light. The prophet Isaiah writes, "The people that walked in darkness have seen a great light. On those who lived in the land of deep shadow, a light has shone." (Isaiah 9.1) Jesus is the light of the world. He changes the darkness of our sin, doubt and unbelief into the light of faith, hope and love. That is why we pray, "Come, Lord Jesus."

The appearance of Jesus on the road to Emmaus

Luke's account of this appearance of the risen Jesus differs in several ways from his other appearances to the disciples.

- The Emmaus couple are ordinary people who followed Jesus. They are troubled; they cannot understand why Jesus has left them in the lurch after all they were led to expect of him.

- At first, the travellers do not recognize Jesus; but once they do recognize him they do not hesitate to believe. The apostles, on the other hand, do recognize Jesus but they do not believe the evidence of their senses. They take some time to be convinced - Jesus eats with them and invites doubting Thomas to touch his wounds.

- In the Emmaus story, Jesus disappears as soon as he is recognized. The other appearances of Jesus were generally quite extended. Sometimes he instructed his disciples at length - for example, when he appeared in the upper room where they were hiding, or prepared a breakfast for them after a night's fishing.
(John 20.19 - 25; 21.9 - 13)

The Emmaus story and the Eucharist

The early Christian community may have written this account of Our Lord's appearance in such a way that it becomes a kind of parable on the way Jesus comes to us in the Eucharist at Mass; the sequence of events follows the outline structure of the Mass itself.

- **Jesus joins the travellers on the road.**
  Jesus joins us in the parish community.

- **Jesus opens their hearts to the scriptures.**
  Jesus speaks to our hearts as we listen to the Word of God.

- **Jesus showed how his sacrifice on Calvary was part of God's plan.**
  Jesus makes this sacrifice present on the altar at the Consecration.

- **Jesus is recognized in the breaking of bread.**
  Jesus comes to us in Holy Communion.

More things we can learn from the Emmaus story

- God knows what he is about.
- Jesus is with us all through life, especially when we are in trouble.
- Jesus waits to be invited into our life. We reply with faith in him.
- Suffering, pain and grief are just a part of life.
- The resurrection makes sense of all our troubles.
- We meet Jesus in prayer; prayer helps get our life into focus.
- Jesus in the Eucharist is at the heart of our Faith.
- We need this bread of life if we are to grow close to Christ.
- The sacrifice of the Mass opens our eyes to understand how much God loves us - just as the disciples discovered at Emmaus.

"Then they told ... how he had been made known to them in the breaking of the bread." (Luke 24.35)

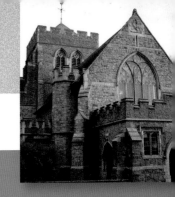

Tabernacle

When we enter a Catholic church the focal point of our attention is the tabernacle. The word comes from *Tabernaculum* which is Latin for a tent. It is a secure safe in which the Blessed Sacrament is placed. Catholics believe that Jesus Christ, the Son of God, is really and truly present in the consecrated hosts. This is called the Real Presence of Our Lord in the Blessed Sacrament. It is this sacred mystery that makes a Catholic Church such a special place. The consecrated hosts are reserved in the tabernacle in a container called a ciborium. The Blessed Sacrament is available for adoration in private prayer, and for taking Holy Communion to the sick. The tabernacle must be given a prominent place on or near to the sanctuary. A veil, coloured according to the liturgical season, may be used on the tabernacle.

In the Old Testament, Moses was given instructions on how to build a suitable tabernacle for the Ark of the Covenant (the decorated casket containing the stone tablets of the ten commandments. See Exodus 25-31). The Jewish faith celebrates the feast of Tabernacles which recalls the forty years when God's chosen people lived in tents in the desert.

Altar

The sacrifice of the Mass takes place on the altar. The death and resurrection of Jesus Christ is made present on the altar under the appearances of the consecrated bread and wine. For this reason the altar is a reminder or symbol of Christ himself; that is why the priest reverences the altar with a kiss and may incense it during Mass.

Early Christian altars in the catacombs were sometimes built over the tombs of the martyrs. The high altar of Saint. Peter's basilica in Rome is built above what may be the tomb of Saint Peter. (Catacombs are underground Christian cemeteries which extend for many miles. They were built between the third and fifth centuries, mainly near Rome).

A tradition developed, which continues to the present day, of linking the death of Christ with the martyrs who witnessed to Christ with their blood. Relics of the martyrs are placed within the altar stone. The altar is called *permanent* if it is made of stone, and *moveable* if made of wood. The relics of the martyrs are usually placed in the centre of the altar surface, beneath the place where the bread and wine are placed for the Eucharistic prayer. The altar is covered with a white cloth and a second, small square of white cloth, called a *corporal*, is placed in the middle, over the relics and beneath the sacred vessels.

Sanctuary

The sanctuary is that part of the church where the altar is located. Traditional designs place the sanctuary at the east end of the building; modern church architecture may favour a centrally placed sanctuary, with the seating arranged in concentric rows. The sanctuary usually contains the tabernacle of the Real Presence of Our Lord in the Blessed Sacrament. Also in this area are placed the lectern or ambo, from where the scriptures are read, and the chair for the presiding priest or deacon. Because of its importance, the sanctuary is often raised above the main floor level and given more elaborate decoration and lighting. Other items on the sanctuary include the sanctuary lamp, seating for the servers and other clergy and a place for the processional cross. Some churches have also placed the baptismal font on the sanctuary area.

Sanctuary Lamp

A lighted lamp indicates that the Blessed Sacrament is reserved in the tabernacle. The lamp may be wall mounted or suspended from the ceiling in the sanctuary area. It is sometimes inside a red-tinted glass container. The colour has no liturgical significance. The only time the lamp is absent is after the Maundy Thursday evening Mass of the Lord's Supper until the first Mass of Easter on Holy Saturday night.

Altar Breads

This is the name given to the bread which will be consecrated at Mass. Once consecrated, it is called the *sacred host*. Size and shape vary according to local custom. In the U.K most are small and round. They are made from unleavened bread - only wheat flour and water. Jesus used unleavened bread at the Last Supper because it was a Passover meal. Gluten-free altar breads are available for those with a wheat allergy. These are usually square in shape to avoid confusion.

Altar Wine

The wine used at Mass must be 'natural and pure grape wine'. In the time of Our Lord, it was customary to dilute the wine with a little water. Now, a few drops of water are added to the chalice at Mass. This symbolises our desire that "we may come to share in the divinity of Christ, who humbled himself to share in our humanity."

Baptismal Font

This is a bowl or container where the sacrament of Baptism is administered. It may be located in a separate side chapel or baptistery or near the church entrance. If it is located on the sanctuary, it enables the whole community to see and welcome a new member of the community of faith.

Candles

Candles were first used in the early church, not only to give light for prayer but as an offering and sign of respect and veneration at the tombs of the martyrs. Today, candles are much in use in the public liturgy and in private devotions. They remind us that Jesus Christ, the Light of the World, is risen from the dead. We celebrate this at the Easter Vigil when we enter the darkened church with candles lit from the newly blessed and lighted Easter candle.

Candles accompany the processional cross at the beginning and end of all solemn liturgies. They are carried in procession with the book of the Gospels at Mass, and also in procession with the Blessed Sacrament on the feast of the Body and Blood of Christ and at the Good Friday celebration of the Lord's Passion. A single candle is placed either side of or near to the altar at Mass. Candles are used at Benediction and for periods of Eucharistic adoration. Candles are also used at Baptism when the parent or godparent, on behalf of the child, receives the light of Christ from the Easter candle.

confessional   chair
processional cross
crucifix

Paschal Candle

This is the large Easter candle, symbolising the risen Christ, the Light of the World, which is blessed at the beginning of the Easter Vigil liturgy. Five grains of incense, contained in brass studs, are inserted into the candle to remind us of the five wounds of Christ on the cross. The candle is inscribed with the current year and the first and last letters of the Greek alphabet (*Alpha and Omega*) to remind us that Jesus Christ is the beginning and end of all things. After the solemn announcement of Easter, the paschal candle is placed near the lectern until Pentecost. For the rest of the year it is placed near the baptismal font. The paschal candle is used at both baptisms and funerals to remind us that Christ is risen from the dead, shares his life with us in the sacraments and promises new life at the resurrection.

Votive Candles

Votive candles are usually small wax lights or candles which are lit and placed near a statue of the Sacred Heart, of Our Lady or one of the other saints. They are simple signs of our love and devotion. We light them when we ask for special help for ourselves or others, or when we wish to give thanks for the favours and blessings we have received.

The burning candle is a symbol of Christ's love for us. Just as a candle is steadily consumed as it gives out its light and warmth, so also our Lord Jesus gave up his life in loving atonement for our sins. Each candle also gives the same light, whatever its size, colour or shape. This reminds us that we are all equally precious in the sight of God.

Confessional

The confessional is the place where we celebrate the Sacrament of Penance. It may also be known as the Reconciliation room. There are two ways of going to confession. The first is when we speak to the priest face to face. This is sometimes called *open confession*. It is often in a quiet, open part of the church or school. Other people can see us but cannot hear what is being said. The second way is when we speak to the priest in private in a small room in the church called a *confessional box*. It is divided by a screen, partition or curtain. The priests sits on one side and there is a chair or kneeler on the other. The priest can hear what we say but cannot see who we are.

Both ways of going to confession are completely secret; the only real difference is the use of the private room. Most confessionals will be fitted with a glass-panelled, sound-proof door. This allows both penitent and priest to be seen, without their conversation being overheard.

Confessions can be heard almost anywhere - in private houses or nursing homes, in hospitals or prisons, in the open air during pilgrimages or retreats, on public transport, in the street or on the field of battle.

President's chair

The president's chair is the seat on the sanctuary which is reserved for the priest who leads the community in prayer and presides over the liturgy, The priest receives his authority from the Bishop. The bishop's chair in his cathedral is more elaborate, reflecting his responsibilities for the diocese. The Greek word for chair is *Cathedra*, from which we get the word Cathedral. The cathedral is the main church in the diocese.

Consecration crosses and candles

New churches are solemnly blessed and dedicated to the worship of God in a ceremony known as *consecration*. As part of the ceremony, the bishop anoints the walls in twelve places with the sign of the cross. The places are marked by some form of fixed cross, in wood, metal or stone as a reminder that the faith of the church rests on the faith of the twelve apostles. Above each cross there is a candle holder, and lighted candles are placed in them on the anniversary day of the church's consecration and on other major feast days.

Processional cross

The processional cross or crucifix is mounted on a pole or staff and carried at the front of liturgical processions, immediately behind the thurifer. It is a symbol of our faith. The cross bearer may be accompanied by two candle bearers called acolytes.

Crucifix

Every Catholic church has a cross either fixed to the east wall of the sanctuary or suspended above the altar, on which is the figure of our crucified Lord. This is called a *crucifix*. It is one of the most familiar objects of Catholic devotion. It reminds us that Jesus died on the cross for our sins. Catholics often carry a rosary which has a small crucifix attached to it. Some people wear a crucifix or cross on a chain around their neck. Regrettably, this has become a fashion accessory rather than a profession of Christian faith.

In the early church, one would not have found a crucifix at all. The horror and shame of this form of execution discouraged the early Christians from depicting our Lord's death in this shocking way. When eventually the crucifix was introduced, about the 5th century, the figure on the cross was not that of a corpse but rather that of a living person - Christ in glory. Vividly aware of the living presence of Jesus, the early Christians depicted him on the cross as having already risen from the dead. He was resplendent in royal robes - very much a glorified and triumphant victor over sin and death.

The Cross and Resurrection

It was this very claim - that Jesus is risen from the dead - that formed the main element in the early preaching of the apostles. We call this early summary of the gospel message the *Kerygma* (Greek for *proclamation*). In Acts of Apostles, after the Holy Spirit had come upon the apostles at Pentecost, Peter's main message to the people was that Jesus Christ is alive! Details of Peter's preaching are recorded in Acts 2.14-39 and 3.12-26.

During the afternoon liturgy on Good Friday, there is a solemn entry of the cross. The priest announces, "This is the wood of the cross on which hung the saviour of the world." The people are then invited to venerate this symbol of our redemption. Although the cross itself is the focus of our attention, many churches use a large crucifix and the faithful will usually bow, touch or kiss the figure of the crucified Christ.

"I am the light of the world.   Whoever follows me will never walk in darkness." (John 8.12)

Cruets

Cruets are the containers used for wine and water at Mass. They are made from glass, metal or porcelain. They may be brought to the altar in the offertory procession, together with the altar breads. Sunday Masses in large churches may also require the use of larger carafes to contain the wine.

Bells

All churches have either a small hand bell or a gong on the sanctuary which is sounded at the Consecration and Communion. Some churches ring (or toll) one or more large bells to announce the celebration of Mass, weddings and funerals. This practice dates back to the sixth century and had a practical purpose long before clocks became common. Church bells were used to announce the beginning and end of the working day.

One traditional Catholic custom is called *Ringing the Angelus*. This reminds us to pray to our Blessed Lady. The angelus is rung three times a day, at 6.am, 12.00 midday and 6.pm. The chimes consist of a simple pattern of three groups each of three single strokes of the bell followed by a group of nine.

Some churches still maintain this custom and it is a happy reminder of the days the Catholic Faith was part of people's lives. Other churches play popular hymns. The use of skilled bell ringers is rare in Catholic churches. Few can afford even a modest peal of bells; others ring their bells by an electric mechanism. However the art and technique of campanology is still practised with great skill and to wonderful effect in some Anglican churches and cathedrals.

Thurible

This is a metal bowl which contains burning charcoal, on which incense is placed to create scented smoke. It can be free standing but it is more usually suspended from chains. The server responsible for carrying the thurible is called the *thurifer*. He or she leads the procession swinging the thurible, in front of the processional cross or the book of the gospels. The thurible may also be called a *censer*.

Incense

This is a powdered resin extracted from (mainly eastern) plants and trees. It gives off a scented smoke when burned in the thurible. Incense is used as a symbol, a simple gesture with a deeper meaning. Here it reminds us of prayer rising to God. At Mass it is used at the Consecration to honour the Body and Blood of Christ. The priests and people are also incensed. It is used at funerals to show respect for the body of the deceased. Finally, sacred objects - the altar, the book of the gospels, and the eucharistic offerings - are all honoured by the use of incense.

Charcoal

Charcoal is wood that has been burned slowly with a restricted supply of oxygen. It is the familiar fuel for barbecues; but it is also used in thuribles. It is formed into small blocks of ground charcoal that has been mixed with a chemical; this ensures reliable ignition and convenient use. The incense is placed on the burning charcoal.

Incense Boat

This is a boat-shaped container for the incense that is to be burned in the thurible. A small spoon is used to place the incense grains into the thurible.

Lectern

The lectern or ambo is used for the Liturgy of the Word during Mass. It is a reading stand from where the sacred scriptures are read. The lectionary and the book of the gospels are read from this place. The responsorial psalms and gospel greetings are said or sung from the lectern; so also is the Prayer of the Faithful and the homily. At the Easter Vigil it is also used for the solemn proclamation of the Easter message - the Resurrection of Christ.

Stations of the Cross

This Catholic devotion grew out of the early pilgrims' custom of visiting the places in the Holy Land that are associated with the Lord's Passion and Death. This pious practice was developed by the Franciscans who have care of the Holy Places, and it has been a popular Catholic devotion since the fourteenth century. It is particularly popular during Lent and Passiontide. It cosists of fourteen scenes taken from Our Lord's last journey to Calvary. These are depicted in pictures, carvings placed around the walls of the church or in a small prayer book. The fourteen scenes - called stations - are the focus either for private reflection and prayer or for more formal and structured celebration. This may include processing around the church from station to station with the priest and cross bearer, and pausing at each station for a short scripture reading or reflection, vocal prayers and devotional hymns. Some pilgrimage shrines (e.g. Lourdes) have life-sized figures at each station. Contemporary thought highlights the Resurrection as the climax without which the Passion story is really incomplete. Some churches now include a final, fifteenth station - Jesus rises in triumph from the dead.

Statues

Statues are carved figures of Jesus, Our Lady and the other saints. They have three basic functions: to remind us of the truths of our faith, to help our devotion and to add decoration to the building. We do not pray to statues. They are like photographs, reminding us of the people they represent.

Stained glass windows

Coloured glass has been used in the windows of cathedrals and churches for over a thousand years. They may depict stories from the Bible, especially the Gospels, or events in the life of Our Lord and the saints. They are valuable aids to prayer and religious instruction. They can have a profound impact on a building, create a peaceful space and a prayerful atmosphere, and add great beauty to the house of God. Artistic fashion and popular taste change with the passing of the years, and contemporary piety is not always in tune with the devotional style of earlier times. Current artistic thinking may favour more abstract or impressionist designs; and these can be striking and very effective, although they are not always popular with the faithful.

Chalice

The chalice is the special cup used at Mass. It contains the wine which becomes the Blood of Christ at the Consecration. It should be made only of materials that show reverence for the Sacred Mysteries. Glass and porcelain are easily breakable and are not suitable. The chalice is usually lined with precious metal and, like the ciborium, may be very simple in form or highly decorated. Several chalices may be used when Holy Communion is given under both kinds.

Ciborium

This word comes from the Latin for *food container*. It is a metal cup, wider than the chalice, with a fitted lid and lined with precious metal. It contains the consecrated hosts which remain after Holy Communion has been distributed at Mass. The tabernacle always contains a ciborium with consecrated hosts. This is called the Real Presence of Our Lord. We can make a visit to Our Lord outside of Mass and Holy Communion can be taken to the sick at home or in hospital.

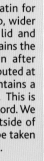

ST. MARY MAGDALENE

Paten

The paten is a shallow dish, plated with precious metal, on which the priest's large altar bread is placed at Mass. Small altar breads may also be placed on the paten when only a few people are present. At the beginning of Mass the paten may be placed on top of the chalice.

Pyx

The word pyx comes from the Greek for a wooden *container*. It is now a small round metal container with a lid, in which the sacred hosts are carried when taking Holy Communion to the sick.

Monstrance

The word monstrance comes from the Latin for to *show*. It is a precious metal container, sometimes of quite elaborate design, in which the sacred host is placed for public adoration. It may be quite large because when placed on the altar it needs to be visible from a distance. The base supports a central stem and a glass display container for the sacred host. The monstrance is used for Exposition of the Blessed Sacrament, Eucharistic adoration and Benediction. It is used also for carrying the Blessed Sacrament in procession on the feast of Corpus Christi, in honour of the Body and Blood of Christ.

Cassock

The cassock is an ankle length black garment with cuffed sleeves and a full central row of small buttons at the front. It may have a shoulder cape. It is the traditional clerical dress, worn beneath the other vestments. It is used less frequently than in earlier times.

Alb

The word alb comes from the Latin for *white*. It is a white tunic covering the priest's other clothes and is worn beneath the stole and chasuble for Mass. It may be held in place by a cord called a cincture or girdle.

Stole

This is a long thin scarf worn round the neck by priests, and across one shoulder by deacons. It is a sign of the priest's office. The priest wears a stole when administering the sacraments and carrying out other priestly duties. It is coloured according to the liturgical season or the solemnity of the day.

Chasuble

The word chasuble comes from the Latin for *little house*, because the cloak completely covers the wearer. It began life as the outer garment worn in the early centuries of the Church by Greeks and Romans. It is a type of poncho or tabard - a large piece of cloth with a central opening for the head. When the priest wears the chasuble he is reminded that he has put on Christ. His priesthood is that of Christ the High Priest. He represents the person of Christ.

Amice

The amice is a large rectangular white cloth which the priest may wear over his shoulders before he puts on the alb. It helps to protect the other vestments and keep them clean.

Chalice Veil

This is a square cloth used to cover the chalice before it is brought to the altar for the Prayers of Offering. It may be white but is usually the same colour as the chasuble.

Burse

The burse is a square envelope made from stiff card and covered with cloth to match the colour of the chasuble. It is used to contain the folded corporal before and after Mass.

Corporal

The word corporal comes from the Latin for *body*. It is a square white starched cloth which is placed on the altar, and on which rests the Body and Blood of Christ at the Consecration.

Pall

The word pall comes from the Latin for a *cloak*. It is the name given to the large white cloth which may be draped over the coffin at a Funeral liturgy to remind us of our Christian Baptism. The same word is also used for a small square of card or plastic, covered in a white sleeve and placed over the chalice at Mass. This protects the contents from insects or dust.

Purificator

The purificator is a small folded cloth which is placed over the chalice at the beginning of Mass. It is used to wipe the chalice at Communion time and to dry the sacred vessels when they have been purified with water after Holy Communion.

Humeral Veil

The word humeral comes from the Latin for *shoulders*. This is a broad strip of coloured material, often white or gold in colour. It is worn round his shoulders by the priest as a sign of reverence when he holds the monstrance at Benediction or in procession. It is also used when the priest carries the ciborium to the altar of repose at the close of the Evening Mass of the Lord's Supper in Holy Week and when bringing the Blessed Sacrament to the altar for Holy Communion on Good Friday afternoon.

Cope

The word cope comes from the Latin for a *cape*. It is an ankle length cloak, fastened across the chest, with a separate, shaped panel on the back. This was probably a hood in earlier times. The cope is not worn at Mass (though it is used at Anglican eucharist services). It may be used at Benediction and Marriage and Funeral services, Baptisms or sung Vespers. Copes are made in all the liturgical colours.

LITURGICAL VESTMENT COLOURS

Vestments of different colours are used for the different liturgical seasons of the year. The chasuble, stole, chalice veil and burse will usually be of the same colour. So also would the tabernacle veil (if used) and any drapes or frontals on the altar or lectern.

White

White is the colour of joyful celebration. It is used for solemnities and feasts of Our Lord, our Lady and during the festive seasons of Easter and Christmas. Cloth of gold or silver are expensive alternatives. On feasts of our Lady there may be blue decoration on the vestments. White is also worn for marriages, baptisms, and (increasingly) also for funerals.

Green

Green is nature's colour of life, growth and hope. It is used most frequently during the year when no specific feast is being celebrated.

Red

Red vestments are used at Pentecost and on Passion (Palm) Sunday. It is used on Good Friday and for votive Masses of the Holy Spirit and the Precious Blood. It is clearly the most appropriate colour for Masses of the martyrs, and is worn also on feasts of apostles and evangelists.

Purple/Violet

Purple is the penitential colour used during Lent and Advent, All Souls day and Requiem Masses. There are two shades of purple. One has a dominant blue shade, while the other (Roman) purple has a stronger red tint.

Rose

Rose is the colour that may be worn on the third Sunday of Advent and the Fourth Sunday of Lent. The reason for this is that the opening words of the entrance antiphons on both days call us to "Rejoice!" This is a small relaxation in the prevailing purple mood of waiting and penitence. This rose colour is often interpreted incorrectly as pink and the available shades of rose are not always considered suitable for the liturgy; some clergy prefer to wear purple.

Black

Black is very rarely used for vestments nowadays; but it remains an optional colour for All Souls day and Requiem Masses.

Blue

In Spain, by special permission, blue vestments may be worn on feasts of Our Blessed Lady.

Holy Water Font

When Catholics come into church, we dip our fingers into the blessed water and make the sign of the cross. This is called *blessing ourselves*. It means that we are renewing our commitment to follow Christ. This commitment was first made for us by our parents and godparents at our Baptism. The holy water is contained in a small bowl, called a font or stoup, fixed to the wall near the entrance to the church.

FAITH SYMBOLS

IHS

This is an abbreviation - the first three letters - of the Greek word for *Jesus*. The IHS symbol was often used by the fifteenth century Italian saint Bernardine of Siena to publicise devotion to the holy name of Jesus. This early use of a religious logo has resulted in his becoming the patron of advertisers. Over the centuries, popular tradition incorrectly attributed other meanings to this simple monogram. The IHS symbol may be embroidered on chasubles and copes to remind us that the priest ministers in the name of Christ.

XR - The Chi Ro Symbol

This is an abbreviation - the first two letters - of the Greek word for Christ. In Greek these two letters are written as a large X and P. Like the IHS monogram, the Chi Rho symbol is used on vestment and sacred vessels.

AMDG

This is an abbreviation of the Latin expression *ad majorem Dei gloriam*. It means 'For the greater glory of God.' It is sometimes printed in books or marked on religious objects as a sign that they are offered in faith and devotion to Almighty God.

INRI

Most crucifixes have this inscription fixed above the figure of Christ. It is an abbreviation of the Latin inscription *Iesus Nazarenus Rex Iudaeorum*. It means 'Jesus the Nazarene, King of the Jews.' In Saint John's Gospel (19.19) we read that Pontius Pilate had this statement fixed to the cross on which Jesus died. It was the Roman custom to indicate the crime for which the prisoner was being executed.

LDS

This is an abbreviation of the Latin expression *Laus Deo Semper*. It means 'May God always be praised.' This too is used as a printed, embroidered, painted or carved decoration and as an expression of faith.

The ICHTHUS symbol

This sign, a simple outline of a fish, is a very early Christian logo. It is still used as a Christian symbol on badges, brooches, or even car stickers. It means '*Jesus - Christ - Son - of God - Saviour*.' The first letters of these words together make up the Greek word for fish, which is ICHTHUS.

In the early church, houses or graves marked with the fish sign indicated that the occupants were Christians. It is a kind of word puzzle called an *acrostic*.

Faith Symbols are traditional reminders of sacred things - just like modern brand logos.

symbols
of the passion
of the evangelists
sacramentals

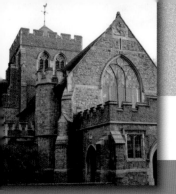

Instruments of the Passion

Some older churches have carved or painted wooden or stone panels, or a screen called a reredos on the east wall, behind the high altar. These usually depict saints or angels, but sometimes they feature the instruments of Our Lord's Passion. These are mentioned in the Gospel accounts of the last hours of Our Lord.

They include the pillar to which Jesus was tied for his scourging, the scarlet robe draped in mock respect by Herod, the scourges, the crown of thorns, the nails used to fix Christ to the cross, the sponge on a hyssop stick used to offer Our Lord the vinegar in his thirst, the dice used by the soldiers to gamble for his seamless robe, the robe itself, the cross on which Jesus died and the spear used for the final thrust.

Symbols of the Evangelists

Matthew, Mark, Luke and John are called evangelists; they wrote the four gospels. An evangelist is someone who announces good news. Each of the four evangelists has traditionally been represented by a symbol or badge. This may be a carving, a mosaic or a painting. Sometimes these are framed by angels or wings.

Saint Matthew's symbol is a human figure, or just a head. His gospel account begins with a record of Our Lord's family tree.

Saint Mark's symbol is a lion. His gospel opens with the account of John the Baptist preaching in the desert, "The voice of one crying in the wilderness." Saint Mark speaks of Jesus being led by the spirit into the desert where he was "with the wild beasts." (Mark 1.13) Hence the lion.

Saint Luke's symbol is an ox, an animal of sacrifice. His gospel starts with the account of Zachariah offering sacrifice in the temple.

Saint John's symbol is an eagle because his gospel begins with a hymn of praise of Jesus who can look upon the face of God, just as an eagle can look at the sun.

Sacramentals

The word *Sacramentals* describes a whole range of actions, objects and prayers that help our devotional life of faith and prayer. They remind us that God is present in every human situation and so we are drawn to pray when we make use of them.

In 1963 the 2nd Vatican Council produced a document, *The Constitution on the Sacred Liturgy,* which described sacramentals as "Sacred signs which bear a resemblance to the sacraments." (60.61) It reminds us that almost every human event can draw us closer to God - and can be called a sacramental.

Examples of sacramentals:

The sign of the cross, the crucifix, holy water, ashes, candles, palms, rosaries, incense, medals, missals, prayer books, scapulars, sacred images and vestments.

Many prayers are sacramentals. These include prayers used at funerals and at the religious profession of women and men, the blessing of throats on the feast of Saint Blaise (Feb 3rd), the blessing of homes, vehicles, ships, planes, places of work, animals, crops and food at table.

Medals

These are small metal discs, mainly round or oval, stamped with a religious image - usually of the Sacred Heart or Our Lady. Worn usually on a chain around the neck, they can be a constant reminder of God's loving presence in our lives. They have no specific spiritual power as such and we should never mistake them for 'lucky' charms - which have no place at all in Catholic faith and devotion.

Scapulars

The word scapular comes from the Latin for *shoulders.* Some orders of men wear a kind of tabard - a narrow tunic open at the sides and with an opening for the head. This garment is imitated in miniature by some devout associates. Two stamp-sized pieces of cloth printed with religious pictures connected by ribbons are worn over the shoulders and under the clothes. Pious practices of this type are now less common than in earlier times.

Novena

As the word suggests, a novena is a form of prayer that is said on nine separate occasions. For example the practice of attending Mass on nine first Fridays of successive months has been popular in some countries since the 7th century. Public novenas usually involve formal prayers said by the congregation and followed by Benediction of the Blessed Sacrament. The Redemptorist weekly novena to Our Lady of Perpetual Succour remains a popular devotion in some parishes. Novenas can be associated with particular days, religious feasts or saintsThere have been several versions of a novena for Christmas. In the 16th century, Saint Ignatius of Loyola, the great founder of the Society of Jesus (Jesuits), suggested a novena to commemorate the Holy Family's journey to Bethlehem. By the 17th century a Novena for Christmas had become a very popular devotion in Italy. This was brought to the United Kingdom in 1835 by the spiritual sons of Blessed Antonio Rosmini..

Devotions

This is a general term for prayers, whether 'private' at home or 'public' in church, which encourage personal spiritual growth in prayer. They are not part of the formal liturgical worship of the Church (i.e. the Mass, the Sacraments and the Divine Office) but they are highly valued by the Church. Novenas are one example of devotions; so also are Eucharistic Adoration with Benediction of the Blessed Sacrament, Holy Hour, Stations of the Cross and the Rosary. One popular devotion is in honour of the Sacred Heart.

Devotion to The Sacred Heart

This devotion has been popular since the 12th century. It was revived in the 17th century partly in reaction to the harsh and pessimistic teaching of bishop Jansen. Jansen's teaching, known as *Jansenism,* taught that Christ died for only a very few chosen souls. Holy Communion should be a rare reward for good behaviour. Jansenism played down the humanity of Our Lord and especially any devotion to the Sacred Heart.

"Sacramentals are sacred signs which in a sense imitate the sacraments." (CCL 1166)

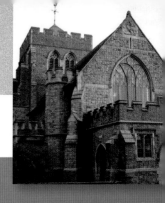

In the 17th century, a French religious sister, Saint Margaret Mary Alacoque, received a series of private revelations in which Our Lord encouraged us to pray to the Sacred Heart. The symbol of this devotion is the heart of Jesus surrounded by a crown of thorns. Many homes still have an image of the Sacred Heart with a prayer of consecration of the family and the home to Our Lord. Novenas and the Litany of the Sacred Heart are a popular feature of this devotion. The solemnity of the Sacred Heart is on June 15th.

Devotion to the Divine Mercy

This devotion has been revived in recent years. Pope John Paul II canonized a Polish nun, Sister Faustina. Her visions of Our Lord once again encouraged us to turn with trust and confidence to the infinite mercy of Christ - under the title of *Divine Mercy*. The focus for prayer is a picture of Our Lord with rays of light radiating from his person. This is a reminder of the blood and water that flowed from the pierced side of the crucified Jesus. At the feast of Divine Mercy on the first Sunday after Easter, images of the Divine Mercy may be blessed and venerated, the three o'clock prayer is recited and there may be Mass or Benediction of the Blessed Sacrament. In particular, many people also take the opportunity to go to confession.

Saints

It has long been the tradition in the Church to venerate men and women who have lived good lives and who are believed to be in heaven. In the beginning, martyrs were venerated as 'saints' by popular acclaim. Later, bishops, monks and religious were added to the list. Over the centuries, abuses began to develop as the shrines of some local saints attracted a lucrative pilgrimage industry. After nearly a thousand years, the Church established a formal process of examination before declaring a person worthy of public veneration. Pope John Paul II further modified this process in 1983. This involves taking evidence that a person has exercised faith, hope, charity and the other moral virtues to a 'heroic' degree.

Evidence of miracles is also taken. This may lead to a declaration of beatification and eventually canonization, when the Pope declares a person to be a saint and worthy of veneration by the whole Church.

Devotion to the Saints

Some non-Catholics are unhappy when they see statues or pictures of saints in church with votive lights burning before them; they confuse this with worship or adoration - which belongs to God alone. It is important to remember that statues or pictures are used merely to help focus our prayer - much as we would carry a photograph of a loved one. Some saints' days are celebrated throughout the universal Church, e.g. saints Peter and Paul. Other saints are celebrated in particular countries or regions.

Contemporary devotion

Many devotions that were popular in earlier generations have lost their appeal for contemporary Catholics. Piety and devotion may have become more community conscious, as the celebration of the Parish Mass becomes the focus of faith and worship, as well as the stimulus for community based outreach to the dispossessed and marginalised in society.

At the same time, we know that our faith needs private and personal nourishment as well as community celebrations of the liturgy. In this regard many still find the rosary a wonderful way of asking the intercession of Our Blessed Lady while at the same time reflecting on the mysteries of our Faith. Some prefer to go on pilgrimage or to spend a few days on retreat. Others enjoy a reflective meditation linked to the music and prayer of Taize.

Music and the Liturgy

The Church has long regarded music as an important element in enriching the beauty and symbolism of our liturgy, in particular the music used at Mass. Since the 2nd Vatican Council, formal church choirs, the use of Latin and traditional hymns have largely given way to a rich vein of vernacular hymns, many rooted firmly in the scriptures, in addition to a wide selection of settings of Mass texts. Some fine hymns are now used by different Christian churches, but discretion is needed to avoid unworthy material.

Many of the hymn texts are admirable but the same cannot always be said of their musical settings. While the pipe organ remains the preferred instrument for the accompaniment of congregational singing, there is no doubt that the use of 'folk' and other instrumental groups has resulted in many attractive settings of liturgical texts. However, these frequently use the idiom of contemporary secular music which some find sentimental, inappropriate, unworthy of the house of God and with little sense of the divine. Pope Benedict XVI has expressed his deep concern about this aspect of contemporary church music.

At the same time we need to be open to new ideas and be prepared to change if we are to grow. There should be room for a varied cultural expression of faith when this reflects the membership of a particular worshipping community. The music should always be appropriate for the liturgy. For example, the Church asks us to sing the Glory to God, the Responsorial Psalm, the Gospel greeting, the Sanctus, the Great Amen and the Lamb of God. A selection of hymns, however popular is no substitute for these texts. The music should have its own beauty, be well performed, sensitive to the size and ambient resonance of the building, and appropriate to the numbers in the congregation. Great sensitivity is needed at all times and a balance needs to be struck between the best of the old and the best of the new. There is plenty from which to choose.

Holy Water

This is water that has been blessed and is used for private devotion or in the liturgy of the church. We use holy water to bless ourselves as we enter church and it may also be sprinkled as a sign of our repentance during the penitential rite at the beginning of Mass. It reminds us of the water of our Baptism.

the church's year of prayer
the season of advent

The word "Liturgy" means the Church's public worship of God.

The Church's Liturgical Seasons

As the seasons pass through the annual cycle from spring to winter, the Church recalls and celebrates week by week the great mysteries of our faith. The sequence of religious feasts is called the Church's Liturgical Year. It begins in late Autumn with the season of *Advent and Christmas*, when we celebrate the birth of Jesus Christ, the Son of God, our Redeemer. This is followed by a short period called Ordinary Time when we focus on the early part of Our Lord's teaching and miracles - called his public ministry.

This is followed by the season of *Lent* which prepares us for the most important religious solemnity of the year, *Easter*. We recall and celebrate the suffering, death and *Resurrection* of Our Lord; his *Ascension* to his Heavenly Father and the coming of the Holy Spirit upon the apostles at *Pentecost*.

After celebrating these Easter mysteries, we return once more to a period of almost six months of *Ordinary Time* during which we reflect on the message of the Gospel which is read at our daily and Sunday worship.

The season of Advent

The word Advent comes from the Latin *Adventus Domini* which means "the coming of the Lord." It is a time of prayerful expectation. We can think about the coming of Christ in three different ways. First we have the historical event when Our Lord was born at Bethlehem; then we can think about Our Lord's coming to each of us every day in our personal life of faith; and finally we need also to remember the time of our own death and the end of time when we reach our final destiny in the kingdom of God in heaven.

We celebrate Advent for four weeks in late November and December. The first three weeks of Advent reflect on the coming again of Christ in glory at the end of time. Isaiah urges us to "Walk in the light of the Lord." Saint Paul calls us to repent before the Lord comes and John the Baptist preaches his baptism of repentance. In the last week our thoughts turn to Mary as she accepts the invitation to become the mother of the Messiah - the Christ child who will be born in poverty in Bethlehem.

The Twelve Days of Christmas

The period from December 25th to January 6th is rich with other special days. On December 26th (said to be *Boxing Day* because it was traditionally associated with the exchange of boxes of presents) we celebrate the first martyr, Saint Stephen. Then we have the feast of Saint John the apostle and evangelist, followed by the feast of the Holy Innocents. On this day we remember the young children killed by the hatred and jealousy of King Herod and we can pray for those mothers who are grieving over babies they have aborted as well as those who have died as a result of violence. This time closes with the feast of the Holy Family and we begin the new calendar year with a solemn commemoration of Mary, the Mother of God, placing all our lives under her care.

The Epiphany

The feast of the Epiphany (Greek for *Manifestation*) is celebrated on January 6th. The date was chosen so that it replaced the pagan festival of the winter solstice when the nights begin to shorten and spring is on the way. Here we celebrate the Messiah who is worshipped as Saviour by the three wise men - representing the wider non-Jewish world. Their gifts of gold, frankincense and myrrh acknowledge our Lord's kingship, his divinity and his humanity. Also on this day we celebrate the baptism of Jesus by John in the river Jordan, marking the beginning of Jesus' public ministry; we also recall his first public miracle when he turned water into wine at the wedding feast at Cana.

"The virgin shall conceive and bear a son, and they shall name him Emmanuel." (Matthew 1.23)

The Advent Wreath

The Advent wreath originated in Europe but reached the U.K from America. The evergreen wreath represents God's undying love for us; the holly represents Jesus' crown of thorns and the red berries the blood shed for us on Calvary. Four candles, three purple and one rose, are lit on successive weeks of Advent. This sometimes takes place in church at the beginning of the Advent Sunday Mass. Some families make a wreath for their family table.

The first candle can stand for the Old Testament prophets who foretold the coming of the Messiah; the second for Saint John the Baptist who prepared the way for the Lord. The rose candle, lit for the third week, can represent Mary who gave us the Saviour; and the fourth candle stands for the Church whom God revisits at Christmas. A white candle is lit on Christmas day to welcome the new-born Christ, the Light of the World.

The Christmas (Fir) Tree

For centuries, the evergreen holly, mistletoe and fir trees had been symbols of life at pre-Christian midwinter festivals when the whole of nature appeared to be dead or asleep. When the 8th century English missionary, Winfrith (Boniface) was preaching in Germany, he found that the Christians had not abandoned their primitive pagan customs. Seeing a child about to be sacrificed to a pagan god under an oak tree,

Boniface chopped down the tree and gave them in its place a small fir tree standing nearby as a holy symbol and reminder of eternal life. He called this "The Tree of the Christ-Child."

This became a tradition in Germany, and Martin Luther may have been the first to decorate a tree with lighted candles in honour of Jesus, the Light of the World. In the mid-19th century, Prince Albert introduced the custom to England (together with the practice of sending greeting cards).

The Christmas Crib

The tradition of representing the Bethlehem Nativity scene dates back to Saint Francis of Assisi in the thirteenth century. Most Catholic churches have a crib in a prominent place at Christmas, a powerful help to our reflection on the mystery of the Incarnation. Many private homes also have a simple crib, ideally made by the children themselves. This can be a focus for family prayers.

The Christmas Candle

Some homes witness to the coming of Christ, the Light of the World, by placing a lighted candle (usually electric) in a windowsill so that it shines for those passing by in the street. This can be a timely reminder for us all and a reassurance for those whose faith may be challenged by the cares of life and the commercial pressures of the Christmas sales.

Who was Saint Nicholas?

Santa Claus or Nicholas was a fourth century Turkish Bishop whose life became the subject of much legend. He is credited with saving three poverty stricken girls from prostitution by giving each a bag of gold, (the origin of the pawn-broker's sign as well as the 'money' sweets that decorate Christmas trees). In Holland, Nicholas became the patron saint of children and his feast on December 6th was celebrated with the exchange of presents. By the time the Dutch had settled in America in the nineteenth century, the legend of Sinter Klaas was linked with ancient myths of the pagan god Thor. Nicholas' home was now the North Pole and he had exchanged his horse for a reindeer, while his episcopal vestments became the red and white outfit familiar in shops at Christmas time. The original legend of Saint Nicholas has no connection whatsoever with the birth of Christ. It has been hi-jacked for commercial reasons and has obscured the real meaning of Christmas.

Mince Pies

The earliest mince pies were small rectangular meat pies with fruit added as a preservative. These were edible reminders of the Bethlehem Crib. Over time the meat filling was replaced by sweet fruits.

Christmas Pudding

In medieval times, the thirteen ingredients in a Christmas pudding reminded us of Christ and the twelve Apostles. Various minced meats, fruits and bread crumbs were kneaded together and boiled in a cloth until solid. It was then served with lighted brandy; the halo of flames represented the sufferings of Our Lord's Passion and the sprig of holly his crown of thorns. A coin, a ring and a thimble were sometimes added. To find one in your portion indicated your future - wealth, marriage or spinsterhood. Mince pies and Christmas puddings were both forbidden by the Puritans during the Reformation.

Christmas tree decorations

Tinsel and instant 'cobwebs' are the relic of an ancient legend. Mary and Joseph were fleeing to Egypt from Herod's men and sought refuge in a cave. A thoughtful spider spun a quick web across the entrance and this dissuaded the soldiers from searching their hiding place.

The Jesse Tree and Advent Calendar

The Jesse Tree takes its name from Jesse, King David's father who was an ancestor of Saint Joseph, the foster father of Jesus. Bare branches are fixed securely in a small container and, for each day of Advent, one of the Old Testament names, printed on a card, is placed on the tree. A short explanation and prayer is usually said. Some parishes include this as part of the children's liturgy. They become more aware of the Old Testament names - Abraham, Isaac, Jacob, Ruth, David, Solomon, Saint Joseph and Our Lady.

A Catholic Advent calendar can be a useful teaching tool for younger family members. Each day has its own prayerful thought to keep us mindful of the coming of Our Lord.

"And she gave birth to her firstborn son and wrapped him on bands of cloth." (Luke 2.7)

the season of lent

During Lent we are called to "Turn away from sin and be faithful to the Gospel."

Why does Lent last forty days?

After their liberation from Egypt, God's chosen people lived a nomadic life in the desert for forty years. These were times of great hardship and struggle, not least against the temptation to abandon their faith in God and revert to the worship of the local pagan idols. Moses fasted for forty days and nights before receiving the ten commandments ((Exodus 34.28); and King David fasted in the hope that God would spare his dying son (2 Samuel 12.16).

In the New Testament we read that Jesus fasted for forty days in the wilderness (Luke 4.1 - 2). He prepared for his public ministry of preaching and teaching by this act of humble surrender to his Heavenly Father. The Pharisees also fasted as part of the strict observance of their tradition. In the early centuries of the Church, the period of prayer and preparation for Easter was much shorter and only gradually became extended to its present length.

Fasting and Abstinence

The bishops of England and Wales stated in 1985:" ...During his life on earth, not least at the beginning of his public ministry, our Lord undertook voluntary penance. He invited his followers to do the same. The penance he invited would be a participation in his own suffering, an expression of inner conversion and a form of reparation for sin. It would be a personal sacrifice made out of love for God and our neighbour. It follows that if we are to be true, as Christians, to the spirit of Christ, we must practise some form of penance."

This is especially true on Fridays during the year. This may include abstaining from meat, but it could be denying ourselves alcohol, TV or some other interest and making more effort to attend Mass, and give more time to prayer.

Ash Wednesday and Good Friday are days of fasting and abstinence. *Fasting* means that we must substantially reduce our intake of food. *Abstinence* means that we must deny ourselves meat or a particular kind of food, drink or amusement. Those who are over eighteen are obliged to this fast until their 59th birthday, and all over the age of 14 are bound by the abstinence obligation.

Lent

The word Lent comes from the Anglo-Saxon word *Lencten* which means springtime. It is similar to our word lengthen. The season of Lent always coincides with the coming of spring when the days lengthen and new life emerges once again after the long, dark days of winter. The Latin word for Lent is Quadragesima. It dates from the 4th century and means the period of forty days of prayer, penance and almsgiving.

Ash Wednesday

Lent begins on Ash Wednesday. At Mass, the priest blesses the ashes and places some on our foreheads as he says one of the following short prayers;

> "Turn away from sin and be faithful to the Gospel." or "Remember that you are dust and to dust you will return."

(The ashes can be made by burning palms from the previous year's Passion / Palm Sunday Liturgy.)

Why do we need to do penance?

We are called to do penance during Lent because we are all sinners; we all turn away from God or reject his love in some way. The Gospel message opens with the call:

> "Repent, for the kingdom of heaven is at hand." (Matthew 4.17)

Jesus calls us to turn away from our sinful blindness and to seek the truth of the Gospel that will free us from our sins. The call to repentance is also the central message in the apparitions of Our Blessed Lady.

During Lent we can express sorrow for our sin by acts of penance, prayer and self-denial. They can remind us in some very small way of the sufferings which Our Lord endured for us and they are one way in which we can show that we want to follow him. Jesus told us to take up our cross every day and follow him. Lent helps us to do this.

What should we do during Lent?

We should begin Lent by attending Mass on Ash Wednesday, receiving ashes on our forehead and resolving to follow Christ more closely. The smudge of ashes on our forehead is a small witness to those we meet at school or college, at work or in the street that we are beginning a special time of prayer and penance. Resolutions should be realistic. One practical way is to try and fulfil our daily duties, whatever these may be, with greater love and dedication and greater awareness of Our Lord in our life. Each of us has our own special path to God and we can travel along it in close union with Jesus.

We may also decide to attend daily Mass whenever possible and give more time to prayer and scripture reading. There may be Lenten devotions that we can attend - Stations of the Cross, Rosary or Exposition of the Blessed Sacrament and Benediction or a penitential service with opportunity for Confession. We can decide to deny ourselves some favourite pleasure or pastime and be more generous to CAFOD. We can make more effort to support our elderly friends and relatives - the sick, housebound and lonely. Finally, we should make every effort to attend with faith and devotion the Triduum liturgies at the end of Holy Week and rejoice in the risen Lord at Easter.

"Jesus was led by the Spirit in the wilderness where for forty days he was tempted by the devil." (Luke 4.1)

a liturgy of enrolment
for confirmation

The Masses of Enrolment and Election are based on the Rite of Christian Initiation of Adults. They should form part of the parish preparation for Confirmation. The first of these simple liturgies is the *Enrolment Mass*, though some parishes prefer the term *Welcome Mass*. It is usually celebrated after the candidates have completed the first two or three sessions. It corresponds to the R.C.I.A. *Rite of acceptance into the order of Catechumens* and it takes place at one of the Sunday Masses. The candidates are reminded of the important step they have chosen and the parish community is reminded of its duty to support the candidates in their journey of faith.

Special readings may be chosen that focus on the call to follow Our Lord. After the Gospel, the priest speaks to the candidates and invites them to state in public that they wish to be enrolled as candidates for Confirmation. (This is not their final decision; they are free to discontinue their preparation should they so wish.) He also reminds the parents, sponsors and the whole parish community of their duty to support the candidates by their prayers and example. The candidates are included in the Prayers of the Faithful. Parishes may wish to adapt and duplicate the following simple outline and make it available for all who attend Mass.

(Name of the Church)
A Liturgy of Enrolment for our Confirmation Candidates

At the beginning of Mass the priest welcomes the candidates with their sponsors, family and friends. He explains why we celebrate this stage in the candidates' preparation for Confirmation. After the Creed he introduces the Liturgy of Enrolment.

Introduction   Dear friends, today we meet in the presence of Christ to welcome and pray for our young people. Some have begun their preparation for the Sacrament of Confirmation. I shall now ask them to stand and declare their intentions.

The candidates may be invited to stand in their places or to come to the front and face the priest across the sanctuary. In some parishes, they present a signed application. Other churches may prefer a more formal presentation to the priest by one of the catechists, with the candidates standing as their name is called. Consideration should be given lest the young candidates feel uncomfortable with such public attention.

Priest: Are you willing to be enrolled today as a candidate for Confirmation and to ask the Holy Spirit to help you witness to your faith in this community?

Candidates: **I am, with the help of the Holy Spirit.**

Priest: Are you prepared to pray, to attend Mass regularly and to attend all the meetings so that you may understand more clearly the meaning of this Sacrament?

Candidates: **I am, with the help of the Holy Spirit.**

The priest now asks the candidates' families, sponsors and catechists to stand.

Priest: Thank you for the support you have given to our young people/candidates. Are you now prepared to continue your support for them by word and example?

Parents, Sponsors, Catechists: **We are, with the help of the Holy Spirit.**

Finally the priest speaks to the assembled parish community.

Priest: Do you accept our young members of this parish as candidates for Confirmation and do you promise to support them by your prayer and good example?

People: **We do, with the help of the Holy Spirit.**

Priest: Heavenly Father, we thank you for the faith and zeal of these young people.
May your Holy Spirit deepen their faith and love for Christ, your Son.
And now, on behalf of this church community I accept you as worthy candidates for the Sacrament of Confirmation.

All: **Thanks be to God.**

a liturgy of election for confirmation

The second of the liturgies is the *Mass of Election*, though some parishes prefer the term *Commitment Mass*. It is usually celebrated towards the close of the main period of their instructions, six or eight weeks after the *Welcome Mass*. It corresponds to the *R.C.I.A Rite of Election and Enrolment of names*. The candidates should by this time have sufficient understanding of Confirmation to want to receive the sacrament. The parish community is invited to elect and accept them as worthy of full initiation into the Christian community. The priest then asks the candidates themselves if they wish to commit themselves to follow Christ. The candidates may be invited to come forward and enrol their names in a special book or present a signed request to the priest. This can be a very effective symbol if conducted with dignity and care. It underlines the importance of their decision, reminds them that the sacraments are the Church's privileged gifts and also makes all present more aware of the sacramental life of the parish community. It is appropriate to give the candidates a token of the community's support for them. A Sunday missal, New Testament or crucifix would be appropriate.

(Name of the Church)
A Liturgy of Election for our Confirmation Candidates

Before the final blessing, the priest speaks to the catechists, asking them if they consider the candidates to be ready to receive the Sacrament of Confirmation. He then asks the candidates if they wish to commit themselves to follow Christ.

Introduction Dear friends, today we meet once more in the presence of Christ to welcome and pray for our young candidates for the Sacrament of Confirmation. I shall now ask a catechist to speak on their behalf.

Catechist: Reverend Father, our candidates for the Sacrament of Confirmation are nearing the end of their preparation. We have prayed and studied together for some time and we believe them to be sincere in their wish to receive the Holy Spirit and to understand the gift which is offered to them.
Their names are ....

The priest now speaks to the candidates.

Priest: My dear candidates, in Confirmation you will receive the gift of the Holy Spirit.
At Pentecost, the apostles were empowered by the Holy Spirit to witness to Our Lord. When you receive the Holy Spirit at your Confirmation, you too will be called by God to bear witness to your Faith in Jesus Christ by the way you live your lives. Confirmation calls you to be a witness, a light to other people, an example for them to follow.

Priest: Do you want to receive the Sacrament of Confirmation?

Candidates: **I do.**

Priest: Are you prepared, with the help of the Holy Spirit, actively to witness to Christ Our Lord and to serve others in this parish community?

Candidates: **I am, with the help of the Holy Spirit.**

The priest now asks the candidates' families, sponsors and catechists to stand.

Priest: We thank you for the support you have given to our young people/candidates.
Are you now prepared to continue your support for them by word and example?

Parents, Sponsors, Catechists: **We are, with the help of the Holy Spirit.**

Priest: Let us pray. Heavenly Father, you sent your Holy Spirit to strengthen the witness of your apostles. May your Holy Spirit inspire and strengthen those who have asked for your grace in the Sacrament of Confirmation. We ask this through Christ Our Lord. Amen.

useful websites

www.vatican.va
Official website of the Holy See. Comprehensive resource for information, news, Church teaching and live broadcasts.

www.catholic-ew.org.uk
The English and Welsh Catholic Church website. Information on all aspects of the Catholic faith and practice. Useful links.

www.scmo.org
Official website for Scottish Catholic Hierarchy. Useful links.

www.catholiccommunications.ie
Official website for the Irish Catholic hierarchy. Useful links.

CatholicEncyclopedia.org
Comprehensive resource on the Catholic faith. Useful links.

www.catholicchurch.org.uk
Supports the English and Welsh bishops in promoting the Gospel. Covers a wide spectrum of Catholic teaching.

www.CatholicDirectory.org
General information on Catholic dioceses, parishes, schools and clergy. Links to over one hundred Catholic websites.

www.cathport.com
Comprehensive guide to international Catholic resources.

www.totalcatholic.com
Helpful source of Catholic news and comment. Databases.

indcatholicnews.com
Information on items of Catholic interest, including books, music and films.

www.ewtn.com (08700 636 734)
Eternal Word Television Network is a global network of Catholic news, doctrine, prayer and discussions.

www.ukvocation.org
National Office of Vocations gives information on vocations for young people. Useful links to other sites.

UKpriest.org
Interactive educational site for young people.

calledtoday.com
The Vocations Sunday (4th of Eastertide) microsite from the National Office for Vocations.

www.sacred space.ie
Ten minutes of scripture - based prayer at your computer. Makes us aware of God's abiding presence with us at work.

www.cts-online.org.uk (020 7640 0042)
Catholic Truth Society publishes Vatican documents and pocket sized, reasonably priced booklets on the Catholic faith.

www.walsingham.org.uk (01328 820217)
Information on the Catholic and Anglican shrines of Our Lady, with details of pilgrimage programmes.

www.udayton.edu/mary/
Dayton University, Ohio, holds the world's largest library of books and information on Our Blessed Lady.

www.maryvale.ac.uk (0121 360 8118)
Maryvale Institute offers distance learning courses on many aspects of Catholic faith. Ideal course available for catechists.

www.catholicsaints.org
Resources and information on saints' names and lives, including suitable confirmation names. Useful links to other sites.

www.faith.org.uk (01737 770016)
The Faith movement promotes the Faith through the media - magazines, books, music, pamphlets, DVD'S, CD's and talks.

www.cponline.co.uk
Lists hundreds of Christian prayers.

www.retreats.org.uk
A comprehensive website listing places for prayer and retreats. Includes Catholic monasteries and retreat houses.

www.cmu.org.uk
The Catholic Missionary Union is a forum for all missionary activities and interests. Links with other organisations.

www.ccj.org.uk (020 7820 0090)
Council of Christians and Jews works to promote mutual understanding by inter-religious dialogue.

www.ShineOnline.net
Redemptorist catechetical material books and resources.

www.familypublications.co.uk (01865 558336)
Publishes Christian and family-related books and resources.

www.ssg.org,uk
The Society of St Gregory is the UK national Catholic Society for Music and Liturgy. Runs a popular annual summer school.

www.cjmmusic.com/shop
Provides contemporary musical and liturgical resources for pastoral musicians, teachers and catechists.

heartandvoice.org
Provides music and catechetical resources for parish use.

www.cafod.co.uk
Official UK Catholic fund - raising Agency for overseas development. Provides updated resources and information.

www.livesimply.org
Inspired by Paul VI's letter Populorum Progressio, challenges us all to face our responsibilities to humanity in practical ways.

www.fairtradeonline.com
Traidcraft and Oxfam have a range of goods at no exploitation fairtrade prices - food, clothing, household goods.

www.carenotkilling.org.uk
Important and valuable alliance of human rights, healthcare and faith groups who oppose euthanasia and assisted suicide.

www.spuc.org.uk
The Society for the Protection of Unborn Children campaigns in Westminster to defend and support all human life.

www.prolife.org.uk
Promotes respect for human life with current information on abortion, human cloning, embryo abuse and euthanasia.

www.cathchild.org.uk
The Catholic Children's Society supports disadvantaged children and families irrespective of race or religion.

www.lifecharity.org.uk (01926 311667)
Pro-life charity providing nationwide practical help on all aspects of pregnancy, infertility and post - abortion support.

www.samaritans.org (08457 90 90 90)
The Samaritans provide a valuable ministry of listening support for those who need to talk with someone in confidence.

www.catholicunion.org
An association of MP's and senior Catholics in public life who promote Christian views in Parliament on important issues.

www.ycwimpact .com
Young Christian Workers brings young people together with a contemporary programme of gospel based resources.

www.faithcafe.org (01727 823803)
Catholic Evangelization Services provide resources for young adult group discussions on contemporary issues.

www.oneworld.net
Works for sustainable development through information and communication. Publishes magazine Index on Censorship.

www.shroud.com
Comprehensive website on the authenticity of the Turin Shroud. Regularly updated with new scientific research.

www.catholicgapyear.com
provides young Catholics with information about how and where they can spend a gap year in a faith environment.

"Today's powerful media can help the spread of the Gospel." (Pope John Paul II)

an outline programme
for confirmation